see
p. 7.

DEVELOPMENT: FOR WHAT?

DEVELOPMENT: FOR WHAT?

Antony Allott, G. McLeod Bryan, Rupert Emerson,

Calvin B. Hoover, James O'Connell, Sayre P. Schatz,

Edward Shils, Douglas V. Steere

Edited by
John H. Hallowell

PUBLISHED FOR THE LILLY ENDOWMENT RESEARCH
PROGRAM IN CHRISTIANITY AND POLITICS BY THE
DUKE UNIVERSITY PRESS, DURHAM, N. C.   1964

*Printed in the United States of America
by Kingsport Press, Inc., Kingsport, Tenn.*

Foreword

The emergence of new nations in Africa and Asia has presented the older nations of the Western world with a formidable challenge, for we in the West are now called upon not
only to lend assistance to the "development" of these new
nations but to justify the kind of assistance we deem most
appropriate. The more involved we become with the problems of the new nations the less assurance we feel that we
know with certainty the direction which "development"
should take, indeed, the less self-evident in meaning the word
development itself. As we grapple with the problems of the
new nations and try to bring them into focus, we may be led
to re-examine and reappraise the nature and meaning of our
own "development." Part of our task will be to determine
what elements of our own culture have universal meaning
and which of our political and social institutions merit imita-
tion. What have we learned from our own historical experience with nation-building that may be useful to others now
embarking for the first time upon that political adventure?

Assuming that our experience has taught us something
worth communicating to others, how receptive will the new
nations be to the advice and assistance we seek to render? It
is not strange that the long period of colonial domination by
Western nations has left the peoples of the new nations in
Africa and Asia somewhat skeptical of, if not hostile to, what
they now frequently refer to as "cultural imperialism." At
the same time it appears evident that they would very much
like to have the technology of the West, and the fruits of that
technology, as soon as possible. Is it possible successfully to

export Western technology without at the same time inculcating in those who receive it the scientific mentality that produced and sustains that technology? And if science must necessarily accompany technology, how necessary for a stable society are other aspects of Western culture?

It is possible that we have something to learn as well as to teach, something to receive as well as to give. As we ponder the meaning of "development" for the newly emerging nations, we may be led to a more profound kind of self-appraisal than we have practiced in the recent past. A world in revolutionary ferment will not long allow us to luxuriate in complacent self-satisfaction. In deciding what we have of value to give to others, we must necessarily decide what we wish to preserve for ourselves and what, conceivably, we may want to discard or change.

The present symposium seeks to elucidate some of the implications of political and economic development. The implications that are seen vary with the perspective of the particular contributor. We have been more concerned to raise questions than to answer them definitively. Though we have not succeeded in answering the question posed by our title, we hope that the essays that follow may serve to illustrate some of the difficulties in seeking an answer to the question and provoke the reader into asking the question of himself. Two of the essays have been previously published; the other essays were written especially for this volume.

In the initial essay on "Nationalism and Political Development," Rupert Emerson argues that nationalism is the very essence of what the rising peoples of Asia and Africa are seeking. "However strong the urge toward better living conditions and economic development, it tends always," he says, "to take second place to the political claims of nationalism." This essay first appeared in the *Journal of Politics* (February, 1960) and is reprinted here by permission. Rupert Emerson is Professor of Government and Research Associate, Center for International Affairs, Harvard University. His most recent writings include *Representative Government in Southeast Asia* (1955) and *From Empire to Nation: the Rise to Self-Assertion of Asian and African Peoples* (1960).

Calvin B. Hoover examines the problem of capital accumulation in an essay concerned with "Economic Reform vs. Economic Growth in Underdeveloped Countries." James B. Duke Professor of Economics at Duke University and a former President of the American Economic Association, Professor Hoover has long been engaged in a comparative study of economic systems. This study has been recorded in numerous volumes, the most recent of which include *The Economy, Liberty and the State* (1959) and *Economic Systems of the Commonwealth* (1962). The present essay originally appeared in the *Virginia Quarterly Review* (Summer, 1963) and is reprinted here by permission.

Sayre P. Schatz discusses the "Implications of Economic Development" and argues that economic development necessarily implies a "transformation in deeply held social values." Now on leave from the Graduate Faculty of the New School for Social Research, Dr. Schatz is Senior Research Fellow at the Nigerian Institute of Social and Economic Research. He has been in Nigeria since 1958. He has contributed articles to such journals as the *Quarterly Journal of Economics, Social Research, American Economic Review*, and the *Nigerian Journal of Economics and Social Studies*.

To what extent is the Western idea of the rule of law incorporated and observed in the traditional African modes of government? This is the question which Antony Allott seeks to answer in his essay on "The African Conception of the Rule of Law." As one of the foremost students of African law, he is particularly well qualified for the task. He has written a book of *Essays in African Law* (1960) and edited a volume on *Judicial and Legal Systems in Africa* (1962). At the present time he is a Reader in African Law in the University of London.

Edward Shils examines some of the reasons for Western disillusionment with the possibility of establishing constitutional government in the new states in his essay on "The Fortunes of Constitutional Government in the Political Development of the New States." Edward A. Shils is Professor of Sociology and Social Thought at the University of Chicago and a Fellow of King's College, Cambridge. He has written extensively on the politics of underdeveloped areas. His most recent writings include *The Intellectual Between Tradition and Modernity: The Indian Situation* (1961) and *Political Development in the New States* (1962).

The conflict and tension between church and state in West Africa are discussed by James O'Connell in his essay on "The Possibility of Pluralism: Church and State in West Africa." It provides a case study in depth of both the opportunities and hazards encountered when Christianity finds itself in the midst of a national revolutionary movement. A Roman Catholic, Father O'Connell has been in Nigeria since 1957, where he now serves as Senior Lecturer in Political Science at the University of Ibadan.

Writing from the perspective of a Protestant, G. McLeod Bryan looks at the impact of revolution upon religion in Africa in his essay on "Religious Developments in Africa." Despite some unfortunate attitudes in the past, he argues that "Christianity has greatly influenced Africa for radical change" and has displayed in recent decades an openness to self-criticism that may provide it with an opportunity to make significant contributions toward the creation of responsible societies in the future. Professor of Social Ethics at Wake Forest College, G. McLeod Bryan is the author of *Whither Africa?* (1961).

The concluding essay of the symposium is written by Douglas V. Steere, a prominent Quaker and Professor of

Philosophy at Haverford College. His essay has provided the
title for our symposium and the questions he raises, though
not easy to answer, are not intended, as he says, to discourage
us from helping other peoples in their self-development but
to suggest that we approach the problems with humility, with
as much concern to learn as to teach, with as much eagerness
to receive as to give. Among other writings Professor Steere is
the author of *Work and Contemplation* (1957).

Although the publication of this book was made possible
by funds provided by the Lilly Endowment, the Endowment
is not the author or publisher and is not to be understood as
necessarily approving, by virtue of its grant, any of the views
expressed in the pages that follow.

John H. Hallowell, *Director*
Lilly Endowment Research Program
in Christianity and Politics

Table of Contents

DEVELOPMENT: FOR WHAT?

NATIONALISM AND POLITICAL DEVELOPMENT*

Rupert Emerson

I f it were necessary to select the most important single force behind the revolutionary drive of the rising peoples of Asia and Africa, the choice would inevitably go to nationalism. For none of its potential rivals can an effective case be made. Indeed, almost all of them contribute in one fashion or another to the mounting nationalist demand. Arnold Toynbee, profuse with capitals, may denounce Nationalism as a "disastrous corruption," "a perversion of Industrialism and Democracy," or "the monstrous outcome of the impact of our modern Western Democracy upon the Parochial State"; but to the peoples newly asserting their claim to equal status in the world, nationalism is the essence of what they seek.

In the debates in the United Nations on the Covenants on Human Rights, the right of self-determination has frequently been considered the foundation on which all other rights rest; self-determination denied, no other right can be secure. It is in this light that peoples around the globe have viewed nationalism, assuming that the remaining goods they seek will flow from its attainment. The usual version of this goal is an acknowledged equality expressed in sovereign independence; more rarely, an adequate substitute may be found in free

* This article was written in 1960 and as a consequence does not take into account events since that time. Nevertheless we believe that the author's primary thesis is essentially sound. It is reprinted by permission from the *Journal of Politics* (February, 1960). [Ed.]

association with another country as is the case between Puerto Rico and the United States, or between British Togoland and Ghana, or perhaps within the French Community before the recent changes in Algeria.

The prime rival to nationalism as a driving force is presumed to be the desire for an improved standard of living. From time to time, it is asserted that the ordinary poverty-stricken Asian and African is really interested only in seeing an end put to his poverty. This is a highly dubious proposition. The evidence indicates that he regards at least temporary economic privation as an appropriate price to pay for national salvation. It has also been contended that his real demand is for a transition to modernity, as manifested in economic and social development. In some part the pressure for economic development derives from the same root as the desire for an improved standard of living. However, it also has nationalist implications in its drive for equality.

However strong the urge toward better living conditions and economic development, it tends always to take second place to the political claims of nationalism. The individual who protects his economic position by refusing to undertake the sacrifices which patriotism demands reads himself out of the community of right-minded, nation-fearing men. As one of the standard phrases of nationalism has it: we would rather be governed like hell by ourselves than well by someone else. Furthermore, the issue between nationalism and material advancement here posed is seen as a quite unreal one since the nationalist creed normally embraces the belief that material improvement will surely follow in the wake of national self-realization. Both well-being and economic development are considered unattainable in the shadow of imperialism. Only when the national destiny is safely entrusted to national and not alien hands is it possible to move confidently ahead on the path which leads to wealth, strength, and modernity. Nationalism opens the way to a new economic era, and the latter in turn lends new power to the nation.

Communism might be put forward as a contemporary threat to nationalism and undoubtedly, in certain cases, individuals and groups have given to the Party a priority which they deny to the nation. More frequently, however, and particularly in the revolt against imperialist domination, communism is seen as an alternative means of reaching national goals. Although objective reality may contradict them, Asian and African Communists are far more likely to view their Party membership as a positive expression of their nationalism than as a negation of it. Official Communist dogma itself puts self-determination in the forefront of its doctrines (even though the small print always carefully reduces it to an instrument to be used for Party purposes) and distinguishes between the rightful patriotism of the unfree peoples and the proper devotion to proletarian internationalism of those whose national identity is old-established. It has often been contended that the success of the Communists in Asian countries hinges upon their ability to identify themselves with the local nationalist cause.

The priority of nationalism has been vigorously affirmed by both Jawaharlal Nehru and Kwame Nkrumah. In his opening address to the IPR conference at Lucknow in 1950, the Indian Prime Minister described nationalism as a war-cry which warms the heart of almost every Asian: "Any other force, any other activity that may seek to function, must define itself in terms of this nationalism . . . . No argument in any country of Asia is going to have weight if it goes counter to the nationalist spirit of the country, Communism or no Communism." Supporting much the same theme, Ghana's Prime Minister cited the motto of the Convention People's Party, which was his own creation. "We prefer self-government with danger to servitude in tranquillity" and followed it up with what he called the party's policy, "Seek ye first the political kingdom and all things shall be added unto you."[1] It is to the attainment of the political kingdom of the nation that the guiding spirits of the new states and their followers have looked, confident that the nation came first and that the rest would follow after.

It is a great deal easier to assert the priority given nationalism than to lay out with any measure of precision its content. Rarely does nationalism represent a coherent and positive body of doctrine and belief, reaching significantly beyond insistence on the establishment of an independent state. Freedom from partition or alien intrusion is normally a far better defined matter than are the uses to which freedom would be put. In the speech cited above, Nehru commented on the fact that a large element in nationalism is negative. "Nationalism is essentially an anti-feeling," he has written elsewhere, "and it feeds and fattens on hatred and anger against other national groups, and especially against the foreign rulers of a subject country."[2]

The negative or 'anti'-character of nationalism in a colonial setting is simple enough to explain, but it is by no means unique to colonialism. Everywhere the national "we" has been to a considerable degree defined by contrast to the alien and opposing "they," and in most instances no operationally significant statement of what the nation stands for can be expected. Indeed, this may be held to be a standard feature of all nationalism until one arrives at what Carleton Hayes called

1. The citation from Nehru is to be found in William L. Holland, ed., *Asian Nationalism and the West* (New York, 1953), pp. 353-354; Nkrumah's statement appears in his autobiography, *Ghana* (New York, 1957), pp. 162-163. In his opening speech at the Pan-African Conference in Accra on December 8, 1958, Prime Minister Nkrumah repeated this conviction: "My first advice to you who are struggling to be free is to aim for the attainment of the Political Kingdom—that is to say, the complete independence and self-determination of your territories. When you have achieved the Political Kingdom all else will follow. Only with the acquisition of political power—real power through the attainment of sovereign independence—will you be in a position to reshape your lives and destiny; only then will you be able to resolve the vexatious problems which harass our Continent."

2. *Toward Freedom* (New York, 1941), p. 74.

integral nationalism or what might today be called totalitarian nationalism. I take it to be characteristic of liberal nationalism that its particular content remains very largely unspecified, allowing for a multitude of sins as well as virtues. The Fourth of July oration of the past, praising America's blue skies and broad horizons, its heroes and its great achievements, reached an approximately acceptable level of specificity. It roused a glow of pride in being an American and yet did not rule out any significant number of Americans who were heretical on one or another point mentioned by the speaker. Tom Paine, George Washington, Alexander Hamilton, Thomas Jefferson, and Andrew Jackson must all fit within the American heritage; New England, the South, the Middle West, and the Far West must find an equal place. If any of them are to be ruled out by authorized fiat we have come to the protofascist phase when some body arrogates to itself the right to determine among Americans what is to be accepted as American. France must embrace the *ancien régime*, the Revolution, Napoleon, and the twists and turnings of the last century and a half. To demand that each nation have a single positive content and program for nationalism is to ask that it select from a diverse history certain strands which alone will constitute its legitimate national heritage. Not far down this road lies the *Gleichschaltung* of the Nazis.

The new states are, however, peculiarly divided within themselves by the gaps that separate different elements in the population. Not only do they have as diverse and internally contradictory a history as do other peoples, but they are also afflicted by an unusual degree of distance between the bulk of the population and the newly arisen leadership. The most notable gap is the one that divides the active, Western-educated, urban group from the inert, uneducated, tradition-bound mass mainly composed of the peasantry. It is the first group from which the heirs of empire have been drawn to constitute the new elite, putting its stamp on the states that

it has been largely responsible for bringing into being. Here
are the makings of a fundamental dilemma. It is arguable that
any nation's claim to a distinctive place in the sun must be
derived from the past that has shaped it in this peculiar national fashion, yet the entire leadership of the new states tends
to be made up of those most removed from the traditional
society of their ancestors. Nationalism has characteristically
been the property of the constantly expanding but still relatively slight minority most influenced by the West.

   The social structure in Asian and African nations, then, is
that a newly fashioned elite, oriented toward the West and
modernization despite its passionate repudiation of Western
imperial control, has taken a predominant lead in societies the
bulk of whose members are still close to their ancestral past.
In such a circumstance, the definition of the national purpose
must evidently be a hazardous process. We do not as yet have
any accurate evidence or body of precedent by means of which
to determine what course the new states are likely to take. We
do not know whether the gaps which are now so apparent will
be filled with greater or less speed, and whether the mass will
tend to move in the Westernizing and modernizing direction
of its currently ruling elite (which seems most probable) or
the elite move toward reabsorption into the mass and the
older patterns of life (which is highly unlikely as a general
phenomenon). Against the current trend toward an optimistic
view of the prospects for development must be set the general
failure of almost all non-Western countries except Japan
to swing into the modern stream during the last century.
Furthermore, the record shows that many Latin-American
countries not only relapsed into lethargy but also made little
headway in achieving the national integration of different
elements of their population. It may be that a similar decline
into stagnation on the part of Africa and Asia is precluded by
the speed with which the world now moves and the new modes
of production, transport, and communication that work to

break down old barriers and isolationisms. The precedents of the past have perhaps become irrelevant in the face of such developments as the deep penetration of virtually every society by Western forces and ideas, the inescapable pressure of outside events, and the presence of communism, ready to exploit every difficulty or failure. Both what has already happened and the widespread expectations for a different kind of future render a return to the old ways impossible. The clear probability is that the West has loosed forces the forward sweep of which can only temporarily be diverted or checked, though no reliable estimate can be made either of the speed of change or of the form it will take. The nationalist movements have themselves been the spearhead of the demand for change.

The existence of great gaps in the society of the new states raises a further question. How real is the solidarity of a nation when it is so profoundly divided within itself? It is evident that no single and all-embracing answer can be given to such a question since the backgrounds and present situations of the different countries vary so greatly. What can be said of Egypt has no necessary bearing for Ghana or the Philippines, and India's prospects may be quite unrelated to those of its neighbors, Pakistan, Burma, Ceylon, and Afghanistan. Precisely the 'anti'-character of nationalist movements in colonial or quasi-colonial countries is likely to lend a deceptive sense of national unity. The fact that a people can stage a consolidated anti-imperial movement conveys no assurance that it will be able to maintain political coherence once the imperial enemy has vanished. It is, of course, true that the mere carrying on of an extended and concerted struggle is in itself a significant factor in the creation of national sentiment, but a more basic identity is necessary if the national unity is to endure. The sense of belonging together through the experience of a common history and of facing a common destiny is not something that can be created overnight.

How much importance should be attached to the gap be-

tween the Western-oriented elite and the mass is not a matter
on which a precise estimate can now be given. When a nationalist movement has gotten into full swing, the people at
large are likely to follow the lead of the active nationalist elite
though they may have given little prior evidence of political
interest. One commentator has remarked that there is no difference between African peoples which is as great as their
collective difference from the Europeans who have ruled
them. When India was aflame with nationalism in the 1930's,
Gandhi and his lieutenants were able to win the support of
many whose knowledge of what the struggle involved must
have been slight. Similarly, when the euphemistically labeled
police actions of the Dutch were carrying colonial warfare to
the Indonesians, an unexpectedly broad segment of the population gave its backing to the nationalist forces. And yet the
gap remains. The mass has so far demonstrated only meagre
interest in taking an active part in day-to-day political life.
The leaders, for their part, have often shown an inclination
to see themselves as an elite, properly entrusted with the des-
tinies of their untutored countrymen. "Guided democracy,"
which Sukarno considers suitable to the present state of development in Indonesia, also describes the elite conception of
government in many other countries. Nor have the mass of
the people up to this point been inclined to challenge the
elitist claim of their new leaders, although the military have
presented a decisive challenge in several countries. Where
democratic institutions survive for an extended time and the
people come to feel that political power is actually in their
hands, the present relationship between mass and elite may
take on a quite different cast.

At this point it is in order to turn to three more specific
topics: the role of nationalism in laying the foundations on
which all further political development must build; the bearing of nationalism upon particular types of political institu-

tions; and a glance at other roles played by nationalism in political development.

The social-contract theorist, in his purer flights of fancy, pictured a world in which distinct atoms of human beings, impelled by reason and other pressures, came together to make a contract that brought state and government into being. In the contemporary scene, the nation-state, as the term indicates, assumes that the state is built upon, or is the institutional embodiment of, a community of men who are already joined by intimate and old-established links. The state is not the product of random particles arbitrarily joined in political co-operation, but the expression of the close prior bonds which has brought this "we" to a sense of difference from the alien "they." Society derives, so to speak, not from a contract but from natural and organic growth.

If political institutions are to be established, a first necessity is that the demographic and geographic limits that define the scope of those institutions should be laid down. In a tribal era they are as extensive as the tribe—which may, of course, be nomadic and thus have no spatial boundaries. When religion is predominant, the religious community sets the standard; at another time the city-state is the accepted unit; and in monarchical days the limits are set by the range of the ruler's jurisdiction. What is important in the latter system is not that a common history has brought the people to a sense of community but that they are all subjects of the appropriate majesty. We are just emerging from the imperial era in which a few of the states of the West, belatedly joined by Japan, extended their political sway to embrace most of the rest of the world.

With the coming of nationalism, all these political systems move into the discard or at least make a suitable pretense of adapting themselves to the new demands. Henceforward it is not a king nor a religion nor imperial conquest nor even a contract that legitimizes a state, but the coincidence of state and nation. Where the state fails to be built upon the nation, there is every presumption that the structure must be redesigned to approximate the ideal. Where empires embrace more than one nation, they must undergo the surgeon's knife, as has already happened in Europe and in Asia and is now rapidly under way in Africa. Only in the Soviet Union, successor to the empire of the Tsars, does the multi-national state survive on the grand scale. Where the state falls short of the nation, as in the partition of Germany, Korea, or Viet-Nam and perhaps in the case of the Arab states, it is necessary to work toward reunification in order to satisfy the present criteria of legitimacy. Given the assumptions of the nationalist age, the first prerequisite is the determination of the national units which form the foundation of the state system.

As it is the presumption that the modern state is built upon the nation, so it is also the presumption that the nationalist speaks on behalf of a nation already in existence. Members of the nation may need to be roused to awareness of their national identity, but national unity itself is taken for granted. To question its existence is almost an insult to intelligence and is certainly an insult to political ambition. The relationships are, however, in some instances reversed. In a great many cases in the past, and not infrequently in the present, it is the state that appears to have been the determining element in the creation of the nation, and at least on some occasions, the nationalists have had to play a significant role in bringing into being the nation whose cause they have espoused.

Over and over again, if the origin of a nation is traced, it will be found that there was a state structure, or at least a political system approximating a state, that coincided to a striking degree with the modern nation in terms of the territory and people it embraced. The regularity of this coincidence furnishes good evidence for the thesis that, more often than not, the nation is a deposit that has been left behind by the state—although this evades the query as to whether the original state itself was perhaps the product of prior ethnic unity. Where the state has survived for many generations reasonably intact within an approximation of the same frontiers, as is the case with France, England (though here Great Britain becomes more problematical), Ireland, Spain, Portugal, Egypt, China, Japan, and certain others, the argument is so obvious as to need no elaboration. Poland, Hungary, Bohemia, and Bulgaria can serve as good examples of states that vanished from the historical scene for longer or shorter periods of time but left behind them firmly established national precipitates.

Outside Europe the role of the state as the formative factor in the shaping of nations is at least as great. Certainly, in the Americas the state played a crucial role in setting the boundaries within which nations were to appear. In Latin America the boundaries of the states tend to have a high degree of coincidence with the provincial jurisdictions marked out by Spain and other ruling powers; and it is the successor states that have shaped the Latin-American nations insofar as national entities have in fact been welded together out of the disparate human materials. In North America the national separation between Canada and the United States can be attributed to a series of historical accidents. Two distinct states came into existence that worked upon their peoples in different fashions and gradually evolved into distinctive national communities. The independent states, which the political processes have created in the Americas, have operated not only to intensify but even to create the feeling of national separateness and identity.

Nowhere is the significance of the state in its capacity as nation-maker more inescapably evident than in the colonial sphere. In some cases, of course, such as those of the Burmese and Vietnamese, the peoples who have recently claimed nationhood had achieved a vigorous earlier communal identity, despite the presence of minorities, and could look back to long-lived state systems of their own. In other cases, such as those of the Philippines and Indonesia, the lines drawn on the map by the imperial power were the determining element in establishing the boundaries within which peoples have developed a sense of national awareness. Here the common government was a major instrument in pressing ethnic diversity into a common mold.

The role of government in bringing to peoples the experience of a common destiny is obviously immense, but the human material involved sharply limits the effect of the forces set in motion by the achievement of political unification. Integration is possible where peoples have an original similarity and may be totally or virtually excluded where they are divided by large-scale disparities in such basic elements as race, culture, religion, and language. Thus the closely related native communities of the Indonesian Archipelago lent themselves easily to assimilation into a general national pattern when they were brought under a single roof by Dutch rule, although the scattered islands and the divisive nature of the Dutch system made national unity a somewhat tenuous matter. The Chinese in Indonesia, however, presented almost insuperable barriers to any comparable assimilation. Immense difficulties obviously attended the effort to bring about a national consolidation of the Malays, Chinese, and Indians in Malaya, and there is good reason to assume that no government would have been able to merge the Arabs and Jews of Palestine. In such instances the bonds of prior communal attachment were too deeply rooted and the differences between the peoples too profound. Similarly, in Africa through the superimposition of a colonial government, a group of African tribes may achieve a sense of national identity in which Europeans and Indians living under the same government are highly unlikely to share, despite the brave slogans of partnership. The effectiveness of the state in forging a nation dwindles away to the vanishing point in such a situation as that of South Africa where the *apartheid* doctrine explicitly rejects any conception of building a single national community. The introduction of communalism, as in India and East Africa, also serves as an obstacle.

One case which is peculiarly complex and perennially absorbing is that of India. Here a vast subcontinent, a Europe in itself, characterized by a diversity of languages, religions, and patterns of life, achieved over the millennia some feeling, however loose and ill-defined, that all the diversities had their place in a single whole. This amorphous spiritual identity had found virtually no expression in political unity: the characteristic political condition was a shifting array of states and principalities, conquests and alliances, lending color to the trite comment that India was only a geographical expression. Whether India would have established itself as a consolidated nation-state or disintegrated into a plurality of states and peoples if the British had not taken over is a speculation in the blue which is entertaining but unanswerable. Certainly it is evident that the effect of British rule—plus modern innovations in transport and communications—in promoting a working sense of Indian unity was of vital importance. The maintenance of law and order, administrative unity, the introduction of a common body of social and political concepts and values, the appearance of English as a *lingua franca*, fiscal and economic integration, all served to link together the disparate elements which made up the Indian society—as did the common national struggle against British rule. At least for the newly rising leaders who created the nationalist movement, the fact of a common British background, as well as of a common British enemy, seems almost as important as the common Indian heritage. When India secured independence, the British trained and educated elements dominated the scene—British trained and educated even though many of them had spent much of their lives in British jails—and the Indian Civil Service, one of the most strikingly successful products of the British connection, carried on the administration through the first difficult years.

Despite the generally unifying effect of British rule, the last turn of the wheel brought not unity but partition. This is an irrefutable demonstration, confirmed also by Ireland's partition, that a single political system does not necessarily bring political unification in its train. Whether the cause be assigned to the divide-and-rule Machiavellianism of the British, to the irreconcilable original cleavage between Hindu and Muslim finding new expression under changed conditions, or to more ephemeral and accidental elements such as the character of Gandhi or the role and ambitions of Jinnah, the fact remains that from one British India there emerged two independent states, each endowed with its own variant of nationalism.

For other Asian territories, the effect of the era of colonialism was less marked both because the duration of colonial rule was briefer and because the ethnic identity of the peoples had already been well established. Since Korea, for example, had an ancient heritage of independent existence under its own rulers, Japanese domination served less as a unifying force than a stimulant to national awareness and political action. In Indochina much the same was true for the Vietnamese and Cambodians, both of which peoples look back to long centuries of separate, if checkered, existence. In setting up a federal rather than a unitary structure, the French colonial regime took these differences explicitly into account. It went beyond them in its tripartite division of Viet-Nam without succeeding in breaking up the unity of the Vietnamese people, although the latter were destined to undergo a new partition at the end of the French era.

Africa, south of the Sahara, offers a terrain in which a unique opportunity to bring nations into being is given to the nationalist and to the state, the latter appearing usually in the guise of a colonial administration. Elsewhere in the world, the determinants of national allegiance can often be traced back to a remote past, and reasonably fixed landmarks of history, culture, and religion separate one nation from another. In Africa such national landmarks are at best much less evident and clearcut and at worst have as yet not come into visible existence at all. The precolonial history of the continent had its quota of internal wars, conquests, and empires, but their effect in integrating large masses of people into potentially national communities was markedly more limited than in other parts of the world. The clan and the tribe, varying greatly in size in different parts, have been, and in large measure remain, the typical social and cultural units. If nations are to appear, they are still for the most part in the making. As to what the decade or two ahead may hold in the way of unification and division of African peoples, I believe that a glance into any one crystal ball is about as good as another.

For the moment, however, Africa is the continent par excellence to sustain the thesis that colonial governments, given appropriate circumstances, may be the major instruments in shaping nations. In the first round, political demands are directed to the colonial authorities, and the implicit or explicit assumption is likely to be made that since "national self-determination" is what the contemporary world expects, anticolonial movements assume the title of nationalism and are assumed to be serving as the agents of nations.

On the face of it, the current drift has unquestionably been toward a new territorial nationalism in Africa which takes the existing colonies as setting the frame of political reference. The caveat should, however, immediately be added that the cases on which we can generalize as to the relations between colonies and African nations are still so few in number, so limited in time, and so uncertain in their bearing, as to make any generalization immediately suspect. It is, in fact, nearer the truth to assert that there are as yet no coherent nations in

sub-Saharan Africa than to claim that each of the political
jurisdictions has shaped a nation within its ethnically arbitrary frontiers. Even among the whites of South Africa, the
Afrikaner has been by no means prepared to accept absorption
into a single South African nation with his British-descended
countrymen. As the oldest of the African states, Ethiopia embraces wide ethnic diversity and Liberia remains deeply divided between the Africans of the hinterland and the descendants of the settlers from America, even though significant
efforts have been made of late to bring the two within a common framework. The Sudan and Ghana, in their different
fashions, are likewise made up of heterogeneous elements that
only much patience, time, and tactful labor can weld together.
Nigeria is notoriously a precarious lumping-together of
peoples whose separate identity is at least as real a matter as
their acceptance of national unity.

The French colonial territories present an even more baf-
fling picture of national ambiguity. The British system, despite its fondness for indirect rule which maintains a particularistic tribal solidarity, tends to produce a measure of
identification with the territory concerned. The French system has operated in a much more diffuse fashion. With Paris
as its all-absorbing center and with central political institutions in which Africans were represented, the local territorial
community and institutions tended to be lost from sight.
Furthermore, the vast African holdings of France were divided into the two large federations of West and Equatorial
Africa, the former of which had eight and the latter four
provincial subdivisions. A substantial number of alternatives
presented themselves. Was the unit of ultimate national allegiance to be the total Franco-African community, as some
French spokesmen were given to assert, or the whole of French
Africa, or each of the two federations, or the individual territories within the federations, or some other grouping of these
territories based, perhaps, on still continuing tribal ties? A

huge amount of jockeying for position and of more basic community formation obviously lies ahead, in the course of which the kinds of political allegiance that will dominate the future and determine the drawing of the new African frontiers will gradually become clear.

The uncertainties of the present situation can be illustrated on every side. The independence of Guinea, for example, suddenly asserted at the time of the referendum of the De Gaulle constitution, carried no necessary implication that the new state represented a national entity, and the decision to join forces with Ghana in some undesignated fashion again changed the terms of reckoning. At recent African conferences and in the pronouncements of leading spokesmen, much has been heard of the existence of an "African personality" and of Pan-Africanism or of some merger of West African territories. The one constant factor in the situation is that Africa is caught up in a ferment of change and political upheaval, whose end is not yet in sight and whose ultimate form is still subject to a great measure of variation. Neither the older tribal units nor the present colonial boundaries are likely to furnish the full blueprint of the future, and it is even more unlikely that any grandiose conception of a consolidated Pan-African union will be created in any foreseeable future. The establishment of a number of separate and independent states, each of which will have its own body of vested interests and distinctive features, will work to make mergers increasingly difficult, but a number of present colonial jurisdictions seem palpably unviable and must seek to join forces with neighboring areas.

In Nigeria and Tanganyika, in the Congo, Guinea, and Equatorial Africa, the European powers have been engaged in a process that has a great bearing on the formation of nations, whether or not nations directly emerge from the colonial regimes which are now one by one vanishing. The work of the colonial administrators is actively supplemented by

that of the nationalists, who, in Africa even more than elsewhere, may claim the title of nation builders as well as political leaders. Everywhere the nationalists are by definition in
the forefront of the national movements, and they are assumed
to have a more acute awareness of its existence than the
ordinary man, but it is also assumed that their role is not that
of creating the nation but of rousing it to consciousness. The
nation is something that is there as a great historical fact; it
requires only the appropriate circumstances and the appeal of
the leaders to swing it into political action. The task of the
men of mid-nineteenth-century Germany, Meiji Japan, or
early twentieth-century Egypt was not to forge disparate elements into a hitherto non-existent identity but to give full
expression to the deep underlying sense of national community that generations of living together had produced.

In Africa this approach to the national issue is in great part
an illusion. It may, indeed, be argued with only slight exag-
geration that the nations so far exist only in the persons of the
nationalists themselves since they are the only people who
have moved beyond the tribal horizons and have come to a
broader sense of the society in which they live. The mass of
the population in whose name they claim to speak continues
to be divided into tribes that are bound together by little, if
anything, in the way of language, religion, culture, or shared
historical experience. The one common aspect of their lives
has been the brief period of subjection to European rule, and
this, for the bulk of them, has often meant virtually nothing
in the way of a common life. Formally speaking, they have
been under a common government with its uniform economy
and system of law and administration, but in practice they
have lingered very largely within the framework of their
traditional societies and have perhaps only recently been
brought into any significant degree of association with their
fellow colonials. As a random sample of what is involved, one
might cite the comment of James S. Coleman in 1956 that

"until the last five years the overwhelming majority of the peoples of northern Togoland were unaware of the existence of Togoland."[3] In the African setting, the nationalists speak for nations yet to be born and themselves have a great responsibility for their emergence. Anticolonialism may serve as a rallying-cry to build up a popular front of resistance, but the constructive work of bringing forth nations out of a motley colonial assemblage of tribes still remains almost wholly a matter for the future even after sovereign independence has been achieved.

The nation establishes the demographic and geographic frontiers of the state. For the survival of the state, nationalism furnishes another vital element in that it supplies the emotional cement that holds the members of the state together when disagreements threaten to pull them apart. What the social contract sought to provide by engaging men in formal obligations to each other came to be provided in the contemporary world by the social-historical fact of being born, brought up, and educated within the close-knit and emotion-laden confines of the nation. In the theory of the national era, the state exists in order to realize the purposes of the nation, and, short of external attack, it can maintain its unity as long as the "we" of the nation takes priority over all the divergent pulls which might distract and disrupt.

Does nationalism have a clear tendency to produce one or another type of political institution? The answer to this question must be a slightly hesitant "no," slightly hesitant because nationalism has in it democratic elements which cannot be ignored even where it has turned in ruthlessly authoritarian directions.

In fact, to assign to nationalism any particular political coloration is presumably impossible since it has been associated with almost every conceivable regime and attitude. Even though an impressive case can be made for the propo-

3. *Togoland* (*International Conciliation*, Sept., 1956), p. 5, n. 1.

sition that every true nationalism rests on democratic under-
pinnings of sorts, there are many ardent and unmistakable
nationalisms in which democracy as a specific type of political
system is either nonexistent or is no more than a façade of
outward conformity with current political fashions. Where
the general constellation of forces has been such as to promote
democracy, as most notably in Western Europe and the countries it has settled overseas, nationalism has maintained a predominantly democratic outlook; where the foundations of
democracy have been weak, as in most of the rest of the world,
nationalism has betrayed the democratic promise that the
nineteenth-century liberal saw in it and has become an instrument of the established ruling groups or of totalitarianism. It
is, of course, always the champion of self-government in the
sense of national, as opposed to alien, rule, but it is only ac-
cidentally self-government in the sense of rule by the many
as opposed to rule by the few. Reduced to its bare bones, nationalism is no more than the assertion that this particular
community is arrayed against the rest of mankind. This sense
of separate identity can by itself give no clue as to how the
community may choose to manage its own affairs.

At a time when nationalism in the West has often drifted
in reactionary or militarist directions and when the most
dangerous and abhorrent elements in it have so recently been
arrogantly paraded by the Fascists and Nazis, it may appear
paradoxical, or even outrageous folly to suggest the existence
of an essential bond between nationalism and democracy; yet
both in idea and in actual historical development there has
been such a bond. Hans Kohn has put the matter in the extreme form of saying that "nationalism is inconceivable without the ideas of popular sovereignty preceding—without a
complete revision of the position of ruler and ruled, of classes
and castes."[4] On the face of the historical record, no statement

4. *The Idea of Nationalism* (New York, 1941), p. 3.

as uncompromisingly sweeping as this can be sustained—
and yet it has more than a germ of fundamental truth.

Once full-fledged nationalism has appeared, a transformation of deep and lasting importance in the relations of people,
rulers, and state tends to occur. Even in the fascist variants,
the role which the people play is sharply distinguished from
their role in the earlier type of dictatorship or monarchy, as
witness the efforts of Fuehrer and Duce to carry the masses
with them, to give at least the appearance of popular consultation through plebiscitary techniques, and to spread the
tentacles of the Party down into every cranny of the society.
This, certainly, is not democracy in any acceptable sense, and
yet it is a perverse offshoot from democratic roots. The
Leader and the Party put themselves forward as emanations
of the popular will, as a truer distillation of the national
volonté générale than the people themselves can produce.

To reduce the question to its most basic terms, the argument linking democracy and nationalism would run something as follows. Nationalism is peculiarly a product of or a
response to the distinctive forces which have gone into the
shaping of the modern world. Those forces are inherently and
inevitably "democratic" in the sense that they mobilize submerged elements and classes of society into new social roles,
eat away at traditional attachments and relationships, and
work toward the building of a new great society into which,
in principle, all men are actively drawn. Obviously what is
involved here is by no means necessarily a democratic constitutional structure nor even an immediate approximation of a
society striving toward egalitarianism, although both of these
are likely to be present at least as active aspirations. Far more,
it is the general conception, derived from the changing social
scene, that the people, the mass of ordinary humans, are of
consequence, that they are achieving a sense both of their own
worth and of their right and ability to do something about it,
and that the leaders must speak in their name. The national

era comes to be an era of mass communications and mass production, inescapably headed toward mass politics.

The heart of the argument is the proposition that the rise of
nationalism is normally associated with deep-running social
ferment and change that disrupt the old order of society and
bring about a rise in social consequence and awareness of ever-
widening segments and classes of the people at large. On this
basis nationalism is seen as one of the major and typical manifestations of what Karl Mannheim has spoken of as "the
fundamental democratization of society," the stirring "into
action of those classes who formerly played a passive part in
political life."[5] As the peoples themselves—or, at least, a significant new element among them—begin to come of age and
to a new consciousness of themselves, they demand a new place
in a society in process of transformation. One of the characteristic forms that this demand has taken is insistence upon the
centrality of the national community and upon the latter's
right to make the state the sovereign organ of its identity and
will. The people, after all, compose the nation, and it is not
beyond the bounds of reason to suggest the revolutionary importance of the fact that the social-political community, which
has come to occupy the center of the contemporary stage—
taking over the state in its own name and establishing a new
criterion of legitimacy—should, therefore, be defined in terms
of the people. In the new dispensation, the state could no
longer be seen as made up of the ruler and those who happened to be his subjects, but it became in principle the emanation and instrument of the nation. The forward thrust of the
bourgeoisie in Europe and later of the masses had its close
overseas parallel in the awakening rebellion of colonial people in roughly similar circumstances and under similar
leadership.

The rise of democracy as a political phenomenon has coincided too closely with the emergence of nations as conscious

5. *Man and Society in an Age of Reconstruction* (London, 1940), p. 44.

entities to be explained in terms of random chance. The lines of interconnection between the two are many. The most evident is the one that has already been briefly discussed: the fact that nationalism is one of the major manifestations of the modern social ferment, which overturns traditional relationships and gives new consequence to formerly submerged elements of society.

A second line of interconnection is the immense prestige that democracy has achieved—even among those who have no serious intent of practicing it. Democracy is taken as an ultimate good to which all peoples must aspire but that only the advanced peoples can hope to master. The imperial centers—Britain, France, the Low Countries, the United States—which have so largely set the tone for the world as it has evolved in the last century and more, have established the pattern of democratic supremacy, and they have, at least until recently, made no effort to conceal their belief that the "lesser breeds of man" could not be trusted to manage a democratic system. The imperial powers themselves, properly democratic at home, had to impose a benevolently autocratic rule on the peoples whose tutelage they had undertaken. For the nationalists struggling to win their equality with the imperial masters, here was a challenge: democracy was the political system whose realization would serve as a symbol that the bonds of inferiority had been broken.

Nor was the striving for democratic institutions only a matter of prestige. Assuming the nationalist leaders to be in almost every instance the product of Western education at home or abroad, the political philosophy and political history with which they were imbued pointed to democracy as the form of government that represented man's highest achievement and as the form that modern man naturally adopted. If they lived and studied abroad, they were likely to come in contact with democratic institutions, and in dependent countries the imperial authorities grudgingly introduced installments of democracy at which their wards were allowed to try their hand under close supervision. Political education in both a formal and a practical sense had the concepts and institutions of democracy in large part at its center, and other approaches to democracy were made in the new era through the upcoming political parties, trade unions, co-operative organizations, and other such bodies, all of which represented popular adaptation to the new Western forces coming in under the aegis of imperialism.

Furthermore, a swing in the democratic direction was a matter of vital political necessity for the nationalists. Their legitimacy in the eyes of their imperial opponents, and, no doubt, in their own as well, rested in very considerable part on their ability to demonstrate that they had the mass of their people behind them. If it could be established that they spoke for a nation with the blessing of its people, their moral claim to take over approached the irrefutable. To this moral aspect of their struggle must be added the hard political fact that if they were to represent enough of a political force to have a serious impact on the imperial power whose position they contested, they must be able to enlist the masses in battle behind them. Particularly in the colonial areas, the effective strength of the nationalists rested upon their ability to have a larger hold on the loyalty of the people than could be exercised by the colonial officials. As the grandest example of all, when the Indian National Congress under Gandhi's guidance became a mass organization in the 1920's and 1930's, the British authorities could no longer maintain the claim that the people at large really preferred alien rule nor could they count on having their orders generally obeyed. Prisons and bayonets still served to keep the system temporarily in operation, but they were an unacceptable substitute for consent.

In these and other fashions, nationalism works to promote democracy, but it also contains ingredients that can with the greatest of ease turn in undemocratic or antidemocratic directions. Wherever nationalism is the main driving force, there is the temptation to give priority to the attainment of national unity, strength, and independence. In such circumstances the liberalism of democratic nationalism may yield to the demand for unity put forward in the name of the nation itself. The problem is always present of giving specific content to the national will and singling out those who formulate it. Rousseau's *volonté générale*, itself only precariously identified with the concrete wills of actual human beings, is sublimated by Hegel into a *Volksgeist* that manifests itself in a realm above that of ordinary mortals but must be brought down to earth. The national will speaks with irresistible authority, yet whose voice speaks for it? The national soul may reside in the simple peasant, villager, or worker, but his ignorance and lack of experience of the great world render him, it may be contended, unable to give that soul true expression. In his stead the elite or the charismatic leader takes over as the emanation of the national will. The nation is sovereign, but the exercise of that sovereignty, so the argument all too fluently runs, should, for the good of the nation itself, be entrusted to those who can use it rightly. By this time the national democracy is well on the way toward transformation into nationalist autocracy; and it was down this road that the Germans were stampeded into the disaster of Nazism.

If the nation is one entity with a single sacred destiny, how can it be allowed to dissipate its energies in internal disaffection and conflict, particularly when it is threatened by external danger and is embarked on basic internal reconstruction? In the actual situation of the new states, the attraction of power and the estimate of national need combine to enhance the already strong elitist tendency of Western-oriented leaders who are amply aware of the illiteracy, backwardness, and inexperience of the bulk of their countrymen. And where the civilian elites do not themselves step in to furnish the "guided democracy," the military are likely to be standing by to impose their version of order and of the national will on peoples whose ability to manage the democratic constitutions they have decreed for themselves is minimal. Latin America and the Middle East furnish unhappy models that are already having their imitators elsewhere, often with explicit insistence that the democratic order is being overturned only in order to lay solider foundations for a return to democracy. At the next remove, the Communists will gladly furnish their own improved rendering of democracy.

No great confidence can be placed in the general populace as the defender of threatened democratic institutions. Poverty-ridden peoples, in a climate of rising expectations, are not likely to make their first concern the preservation of political forms and liberties whose meaning is obscure to them and whose promise appears of less significance than other prospects that are held out to them. If democracy fails to produce results with adequate speed and if authoritarian methods seem to hold the remedy, the masses cannot be counted on to rise to the defense of unfamiliar political machineries. In general they lack not only the democratic tradition but also the more basic tradition of standing up to do battle for their rights against the remote and superior authorities who have through the ages pushed them around. Nothing in their experience has brought home to them the belief that they are the possessors of human rights and fundamental freedoms that they are entitled to and able to defend. The present array of democratic institutions has been imposed on them from above almost as much as any of the previous systems; certainly, the constitutions have not been adopted in response to a demand from below. All too often it is probable that the people would feel more at home with a government that, in traditional style, tells them what to do.

Whatever their composition, the ruling authorities in this democratic or postdemocratic age will seek popular consent or approval to establish the legitimacy of their title to power, but this can be handled through the familiar plebiscitary techniques without disturbing the people by placing alternatives before them.

In the West nationalism is now often denounced as being a divisive and anachronistic force—bad enough at any time and intolerable in the atomic era. Of the grievousness of nationalism's faults there can be no doubt. They can exact a high price, yet what is bought at that price is also of great value, particularly, perhaps, for those who are just entering into the modern national phase. The divisiveness of nationalism has a different bearing for new states than it has for those that are old, established, and even outgrowing their nationhood, and the element of anachronism is to be measured not only by the calendar but by the life-span of the particular nationalisms as well.

Even for the Western peoples whose reaping of the fruits of nationalism is of relatively old standing, undermining the nation by insistence on its shortcomings could create a worse rather than a better situation unless preferable forms of community, acceptable to the people, were ready at hand. The brotherhood of man finds much of its present working expression within the nation, even though its other face is hostility to those outside. Whatever changes in the structure of the global society may lie just around the corner, they are still sufficiently concealed to make it impossible to see the form and nature of the nation's successors. We have, unhappily, no necessary reason to assume that if the nation were to lose its hold, the next stage would mark any appreciable advance toward a more desirable world. France presented no pretty picture in the years just before World War II, when the idea of the nation had lost its force for both the right and the left and many in the center as well.

In the newly rising countries, nationalism has functions to perform that it has largely exhausted elsewhere. While in the West the nation has come to represent the actual outer boundaries of communal allegiance for most men or has set limits that are already found too confining, in Asia and Africa the nation constitutes a great potential widening of the social and political horizons of most of the people. Far from forcing men to live within restricted quarters, it opens new doors and windows. Where men's lives have traditionally been bounded by family, tribe, or caste, by village, market town, or petty state, the emergence of nationalism creates pressures that force men into larger communities, as nationalism is itself a response to similar pressures. That lesser communities can put up strong resistance to full absorption into the nation, or what claims to be the nation, is demonstrated on a small scale by the existence in all countries of isolated pockets of people who have not effectively been drawn into the broader national society. On a larger scale, there are any number of evidences of growing pains such as the demands of linguistic communities in India, the revolts in different parts of Indonesia, and Nigeria's troubles with its tribes and regions. In some instances, as in Pakistan's split from India, even the assertion that there is a single nation embracing the peoples concerned may be successfully denied. For many individuals and groups, considerable time will surely elapse before their social-political consciousness expands to the new national limits, but the forces of the modern world are on the whole conspiring to make man's age-old parochialism impossible.

For the leaders and organizers of national movements, it is obviously a matter of the first importance to wean as many people as possible away from their more local attachments and bring them to active awareness of their national ties. In addition to ethical and religious considerations, Gandhi was moved by a simple political calculation in pleading the case for the untouchables: if the latter remained outside the national fold, the Indian nation could bring that much less pressure to bear on the British in its struggle for independence. In taking the national cause to the masses, men like Gandhi, Sukarno, Nasser, and Nkrumah have not only immeasurably strengthened their political position but have also taken a creative part in shaping the nations they represent. All the agitation and propaganda associated with nationalist parties and upheavals dramatize the issues and serve to make the nation a living reality for people who have had no consciousness of its existence. To the extent that the new concept is grasped, the peasant isolated in his village becomes a citizen of a nation that takes its place in the world's councils. The nation is itself still far removed from meeting the needs of an age of jet planes, radio, and intercontinental ballistic missiles, but it is at least an advance in social magnitude over what preceded it.

To the national unity that it brings to the new states, nationalism adds another vital ingredient for survival: a revolutionary zeal and a sense of devotion to the nation and the state that is to be its instrument. In the new states and in those that are in process of formation, the nation is not something that can be taken casually for granted but an exciting new achievement, worthy of love and sacrifices. Independence has been won as the result of campaigns whose emotional momentum in some part carries over and may be utilized in dealing with the problems of the difficult years ahead. Particularly in colonial areas, but also to some extent in any country still living under some variant of the *ancien régime,* the nation and nationalism open the possibility of tapping sources of popular energy and participation that no alien or old-style autocratic ruler could hope to tap. To carry on warfare, to put through major reforms, or to require present sacrifices for future benefits enlists a new dimension of popular support if it can be called for by national leaders as a part of the nation's due.

How long the zeal and devotion will last and how usefully they can be channeled into dealing with the postindependence tasks are questions the answers to which the heirs to imperial power must anxiously seek. Certainly there can be no simple transference. At the extreme the youngster who has carried on years of guerrilla warfare against the Dutch in Indonesia or against the French in Indochina or Algeria is unlikely to be the most suitable candidate for a desk job in the Ministry of Reconstruction and not even perhaps for the routines of a peace-time army. More broadly, the demonstrated ability of the nationalist leadership to perform the political function of rallying the people against imperial domination can give no guarantee of ability to perform another and quite different job. A strong case can be made for the proposition that the sacrifices and basic social changes which development calls for can only be got across to the people by the political leader and not by the expert or bureaucrat, but the nationalist revolutionary who has been victorious in one setting may fumble badly in another. The dramatic and heroic temper of nationalist battle is far from being a wholly suitable mood in which to tackle the problems of managing a stable and progressive polity and a modernized and expanding economy.

Nationalism by itself gives the answer to virtually none of the particular problems arising from the ubiquitous demand for development and, indeed, to very few of the multitude of questions that confront peoples coming to independence.[6] Its most vital contribution is in the realm of the intangibles of the spirit: the restoration of self-respect, the building up of morale, and the stimulation of social solidarity. It does not, however, determine the choice between alternative and often conflicting values, each legitimately put forward as embraced within the national destiny; it does not provide all the good things associated with independence; and it does not establish the institutions necessary for further advance. One must look elsewhere than to nationalism to decide even such over-all questions as whether a free enterprise system or communism, liberal democracy or centralized authoritarianism, is most

6. I have elaborated somewhat on this theme in "The Progress of Nationalism" in Philip W. Thayer, ed., *Nationalism and Progress in Free Asia* (Baltimore, 1956), pp. 71-82.

fitting, and the vast majority of lesser decisions must also be taken primarily on other than nationalist grounds. In almost every instance, to hold up the concept of the national interest as the determinant of decision and action is to produce an empty symbol whose content is in dispute between different factions within the nation. Even in the realm of foreign affairs where nationalism most evidently comes into play, it is likely to give no conclusive answer to questions concerning entry into this alliance or that, neutralism or commitment. The danger is also real that nationalism may serve as an actual impediment to advance, as, for instance, in curtailing access to alien goods, skill, and capital, and it can always be paraded as a screen to hide domestic failures or abuses.

The dimensions of the task that lie ahead of the new states are staggering. They cannot rest content with taking their newfound sovereignty and enjoying it, as they might have at some earlier point in history. Both national pride and the imperatives of survival now demand that they move speedily into the modern world, rivaling the achievements of peoples who have long preceded them on the road. Despite illiteracy, inexperience, and tragic shortages of trained manpower, the latest model of the welfare state plus modernized armed forces is to be produced by governments equipped with all the trappings of parliamentary democracy. Economic systems are to be transformed and the remnants of backwardness wiped from the slate. The new national community is to take its place in the organized society of nations, be represented at a multitude of international conferences and meetings, and furnish an appropriate quota of personnel for international secretariats.

In moving toward goals such as these, nationalism can be of immense assistance if it is wisely and skilfully used by those responsible for the guidance of the new states. If it is used merely to inflame and obscure, its contribution can be disastrous.

ECONOMIC REFORM VS. ECONOMIC GROWTH IN UNDERDEVELOPED COUNTRIES

Calvin B. Hoover

I

Maximum rate of economic growth through industrialization is now the universal goal of underdeveloped countries. Where these countries have recently attained their independence, as in Africa and Asia, the new national governments have held out the prospect of immediate improvement in standards of living as a consequence of the end of colonial exploitation. In Latin America political leaders have offered to the masses a program of reform through redistribution of wealth and income, to be brought about by the overthrow of reactionary, dictatorial governments, which is to produce concurrently an increase in the economic productivity of agriculture and industry. There is apparently no realization that leftist revolutionary governments often turn out to be not only dictatorial, but, in the true sense, reactionary as well. Batista, Castro, and Perón are cases in point. In Africa and Asia, as well as in Latin America, it is taken for granted that socioeconomic reforms will facilitate increased industrialization, so heavily depended upon to bring about the maximum annual rate of economic growth.

The formation of the capital required for this industrialization, however, depends upon restriction of consumption through limitations of wage increases, peasant incomes, and non-productive governmental expenditures. Entrepreneurial abilities and favorable expectations must also exist if the capital saved is to be invested productively or indeed if the saving is to continue. Since favorable entrepreneurial expectations also depend upon a complex of consumer as well as investment demands, there need not be a total conflict between some improvement in the standard of living and the formation of a national capital fund. If private entrepreneurial abilities are not exercised because favorable expectations do not exist, the investment function may alternatively be carried on by the state. The restriction of consumption, just as has been true under Western capitalism, is nevertheless an absolute necessity, regardless of the organizational implementation of the investment function. Yet no government of any underdeveloped country would today be willing to depend upon the historical process by which the capital formation requisite to industrialization took place in the advanced countries of the West.

This unwillingness to repeat the experience of the West reflects the repudiation in most underdeveloped countries of the economic system of capitalism under which industrialization took place in the advanced countries. Thus, the parliament of India, while accepting the existence of private enterprise in some sectors for an indefinite period, has nevertheless proclaimed its adherence to socialism as the economic system toward which progress is envisaged. Egypt, Algeria, and Ghana, as well as most other formerly colonial countries of Africa, have proclaimed their repudiation of capitalism. Indeed, Pakistan represents almost the only exception to the explicit or implicit repudiation of capitalism among formerly colonial countries in Africa and Asia. Among Latin-American countries, which long ago threw off colonial rule but which are still underdeveloped, political instability, together with the current anticapitalist popular movements under Communist agitation, has retarded the development of modern capitalistic institutions and hence the traditional process of capital accumulation.

By the historic process through which capital accumulation took place during industrialization in the West, the increase in national income was made available only gradually to the industrial workers who would have consumed it, but instead largely vested in the bourgeoisie. The standard of living of the new industrial proletariat could rise only slowly during the early stages of capitalism in the West if sufficient capital to permit industrialization was to be available to entrepreneurs. Capital formation by industrial entrepreneurs was facilitated as land passed out of the hands of feudal lords and the monasteries. The capital accumulation essential to support industrialization in Western Europe was a process requiring some two or three centuries.

The chronology and details of this process of capital accumulation varied from one country to another. In England the enclosure movement had simultaneously dispossessed the peasant and provided a future source of labor for the industrial revolution. Thus, in the country which industrialized earliest, the peasants who had previously occupied the land were largely prevented in one way or another from acquiring it. This rental income became available as an indirect source of commercial and industrial capital since it afforded a significant part of the economic base for the support of the state and its ruling class. The capital generated in the developing commercial and industrial sectors by capitalistic entrepreneurs was, of course, of greater direct importance. Conspicuous consumption of the bourgeoisie did indeed lengthen the period necessary for capital formation but was not a large enough fraction of profits to prevent the accumulation of economic resources sufficient for industrialization.

In France, by contrast, the seizure of manorial holdings by the peasants during the Revolution, since it was accompanied by the development of a bourgeois acquisitiveness,

did not increase the peasants' personal consumption sufficiently to inhibit completely the accumulation of a national
stock of capital. Nevertheless, as contrasted with the English
experience, France was left with an inefficient agriculture
based upon small-scale peasant holdings and a backward
industry which had to rely upon insufficient capital resources. Only now, after almost two centuries, are small holdings in France being consolidated by a variety of devices so
that agricultural efficiency can be substantially increased.

To cite Denmark as another example of the process of
capital accumulation as capitalism developed, the large estates with tenant farmers were superseded by the present
system of predominately peasant ownership of small holdings
only in the latter half of the nineteenth century. Nevertheless, some 20 per cent of agricultural land continued to be
farmed as large estates. Denmark represents the relatively
rare case of quite small-scale agriculture developing productive efficiency. Marketing co-operatives played an important
role in making this possible. At the present time, however,
the large agricultural estates in Denmark are substantially
more efficient than the small holdings. Today, the sons of
Danish peasants generally prefer employment in industry or
on the large estates where hours of work are shorter, compensation larger, and the standard of living higher than on
the small holdings. Only stringent legislation against enlarg-
ing holdings prevents the expansion of the larger farms. De-
ficiency of capital for industrialization was not a serious
national handicap for the Danish economy since only in recent times has industrialization gotten under way.

In the United States, abundant natural resources made
capital formation feasible both without the fragmentation of
land holding, which is so likely to be the result of revolutionary land reform, and without such stringent withholding
of income from farmers and workers. At the present time,
the average farm size in the United States is steadily increas-

ing because of the superior efficiency of production of larger farms. This is the reverse of the process of breaking up of large estates widely advocated both on the grounds of social justice and increased output in connection with the Alliance for Progress in Latin America.

Japan affords the most striking example of a country which compressed the process of industrialization into a relatively short period and yet did so without dependence upon foreign capital. During the period of industrialization from the 1890's to the outbreak of World War I, as Professor Gen-Ichi Abe has pointed out, the consumption habits of both industrial workers and peasants retained the traditional agricultural pattern. Rice and fish for food, living in wooden houses on mats, wearing wooden clogs instead of shoes, and the like made low wages possible. Low wages and relatively high output per worker made it feasible for Japanese manufactured products to compete successfully with those of the earlier industrialized countries of Europe and the United States. Exports based upon low wages made large profits for industrialists, and these profits were the source of capital for the mechanization of Japanese industry during the critical early period. This unique combination of the traditional elements of capitalistic accumulation of the West with authoritarian Japanese nationalism laid the basis for modern Japanese industry.

The prosperous industrial economy that currently exists in Japan provides the market both for the products of agriculture and for excess agricultural labor. Consequently, the normal historical order of events has eventually been reversed. One might say that successful industrialization made possible the relative success of the land reform that took place in Japan under American auspices after World War II. The most recent Japanese experience has furnished the rare case of splitting up the size of landholdings without serious loss in productivity.

II

It is not only that there is no sign that the governments of the emerging nations of Africa and Asia are willing to depend upon the historic process of capital accumulation. There is apparently little realization that if the capitalistic process of capital accumulation is not to operate, some other system that will insure the withholding of income from the masses will have to be adopted. Withholding income from consumption for capital accumulation is rendered more difficult by the "revolution of rising expectations." The belief that capital for industrialization can be obtained either by grants and loans from the United States or from Soviet Russia or from both likewise inhibits realization of the necessity for limiting consumption of the masses. There is no possibility whatever that this aid could be large enough to obviate obtaining much the larger portion of the required capital funds out of domestic sources. The very real danger is that economic aid from the more industrially advanced countries will come to be depended upon as part of consumer income and may even inhibit domestic saving and investment in underdeveloped countries.

This failure to recognize the nature and necessity of capital accumulation is the more paradoxical since the leadership of the new nations is so generally influenced by Marxist doctrine. Marxist doctrine held that socialism could come into existence only as the successor to a capitalism that had already provided the essential economic resources through accumulation out of surplus value withheld from labor. Lenin had indeed amended Marx to explain how socialism might be set up in Russia in spite of its being one of the less industrialized countries. It was Stalin, however, who, through the collectivization of agriculture and the policy of concentrating on heavy industry and holding the production of consumption goods to a minimum, effectively withheld income from the masses. Since the Soviet leadership has, however, not admitted outright that capital for industrialization was obtained by this authoritarian mass withholding, it is not surprising that the Marxist-influenced leaders of the new nations have refused to recognize the process of capital accumulation for what it must be under any economic system, namely, the withholding of income from consumption and its devotion to investment.

The fundamental institutions of old-style capitalism, unlimited private-property rights, the free market, and the doctrine of laissez faire, which made the process of capital accumulation in the West possible, are generally unacceptable to the leadership of the emerging nations. This repudiation of these bases of old-style capitalism reflects on the one hand an egalitarianism that is, indeed, largely nominal since the political bureaucracy of these countries rapidly develops into a "New Class" with a standard of living greatly superior to that of the mass of the population. It reflects as well an impatience with any limitation of the power to act on the part of the new political leadership of these countries.

It is no small part of the difficulties of carrying out any program of national saving and investment that the Communist-dominated movements in all underdeveloped countries exhort workers to demand the highest wages and shortest hours, and peasants to demand the breaking-up and parceling-out of estates without regard to the effect upon the productivity of industry and agriculture.

From the Communist point of view, a decline in productivity, or indeed economic chaos, simply hastens the end of capitalism. It is time enough, after capitalism has been overthrown, to see to it that land is not allowed to pass into the hands of individual peasants, or to reassemble peasant holdings into collective farms if temporary parceling out of land has had to be permitted. This is the process which has gone on under Castro in Cuba. There is, indeed, a certain logic in it. As the Soviet writer S. S. Sergheev has put it in respect to the Soviet economic system, "All private farming contains in itself the seed of capitalist reincarnation." Even disregarding their ideological opposition to peasant ownership of land, the Communists are in no doubt about the probable economic results of fragmentation of landholdings below optimum size.

Similarly, after a Communist take-over, there is no hesitancy about reducing real wages of workers in order to obtain capital funds for industrialization, although this may be camouflaged in various ways, once more precisely as in Castro's Cuba. From the Communist point of view, this is quite logical. Although the reduction in real wages is never admitted, its actuality is justified in terms of "sacrifices willingly undertaken by the workers to build up the workers' society, at the behest of the workers' state." This, indeed, differs from the historic process of capital formation under capitalism, where the capital funds accumulated by withholding from the workers become the property of capitalists for their consumption or for further investment. Under a Soviet type of economic system, the capital funds accumulated are at the disposal of the "New Class," which rules the state, and likewise for further investment, to the extent it is so decided. In contrast to the capitalist system, the workers in a Soviet type of economic system have no means of influencing investment decisions through collective bargaining, through the capital or goods markets, or through the election of parliamentary representatives. The "New Class" simply rules the state through its monopoly of all instruments of coercion and propaganda and makes decisions with respect to wage rates, consumption levels, and amounts and directions of capital investment and its own compensation.

In Africa the large landholdings that have been in the hands of white settlers, as in the case of the French *colons* in Algeria and the British settlers in Kenya, are bound to be taken over by the newly decolonialized government if they are not simply seized by the indigenous inhabitants of the area. The income that formerly went to the white settlers, if it could be sequestered by the new governments and used for investment in agriculture and industry, would constitute a partial substitute for the traditional process of capital accumulation. A decline in production is, however, likely to be the result of fragmentation of these large holdings. A shrinkage in the income that the government could otherwise obtain from taxation would be the probable result, not only from the decline in productivity but from the decline in the surplus income above consumption available as a source of taxation. The owners of the small holdings will increase their consumption wherever possible unless incentives for saving can be created. Similarly, there will be a tendency for less resources to be available for reinvestment in agriculture by the small-scale cultivators. Indeed, in the early stages of land redistribution, there will be difficulty even in providing the minimum credit facilities for tiding the cultivators over from one crop to the next.

It has been pointed out by Matthew Kust that in India, for example, the proportion of income from land taken by taxes had been diminishing for many decades even before independence. Even with a fairly sophisticated bureaucracy planning the Indian economy, a substantial sharpening of these problems has resulted from the land reform that followed independence. In effect, the *zamindari* landlords of India had been tax gatherers for the government. Even after deducting the large portion they kept for themselves, it is not certain whether elimination of these landlords will result in a less expensive tax system of withholding funds from the peasants. It sometimes seems that only the free market or something approaching an oriental despotism can withhold income from farmers once they have had political power.

Since not only funds for ordinary governmental purposes

must be somehow obtained from agricultural sources, but capital for industrialization must also come from the same source, this is a serious matter indeed for underdeveloped countries. In the countries of Africa where large white populations had never settled, the economic problems consequent upon redistribution of land are not of such major importance, except in the case of Egypt, where somewhat similar problems have had to be faced. Nevertheless, the necessity for accumulating a national capital fund by restricting consumption is a most serious problem in these countries as well.

Only in Egypt, among the countries that have been decolonialized, does the problem of providing funds for industrialization out of the income from industries themselves yet exist. Here a rather complicated process of partial but substantial confiscation of large industrial holdings, both foreign and domestic, has taken place. It is not yet clear to what extent a simple redistribution of wealth among larger numbers of persons is intended or whether it is intended to retain governmental ownership of the confiscated shares of industrial corporations. As in the case of land, however, the government must resist the temptation to disburse too much of the industrial product to workers in industry if funds for taxes and capital for industry are to be available.

Since the free market of the capitalistic economic system cannot be counted upon in the merging nations to facilitate the task of restraining the income of peasant producers and of workers employed in such industries as may come into existence, the state must do so. But it is likely to be difficult for a democratically controlled state apparatus to take the unpopular decisions necessary and to implement them. In detail, the kind of decision that must be taken involves, for example, denying to the growers of a particular crop, say cocoa, rubber, or cotton, the full value of the foreign exchange that is received from the exports of the crop. This has indeed been done in West Africa, but it is naturally not a popular policy with the growers of these commodities. As another example, it involves denying the laborers in copper mines the opportunity to use their collective bargaining power to retain for themselves the full value of the output of the mines. The absence of some sort of free-enterprise market economy to aid in restricting wages, peasant incomes, and consumption in general places upon the state the necessity for taking this first step in making resources available for capital investment. The provision of potential capital funds for investment to facilitate economic development will be useless if there does not exist either an operable political system or economic organization adequate for the investment of these potential capital funds. If the funds withheld from consumption are dissipated through political corruption, through proliferation of the state bureaucracy and an unnecessarily high standard of living for the "New Class," or through general ineptness, they are, of course, not available as a source of capital. Even if political stability and integrity exist, then state enterprises would have to be set up to carry out investment of funds withheld from consumption if private or corporate enterprise is not to be encouraged to do so.

That these difficulties of carrying out the processes of withholding income from consumption and providing for its investment are likely to set the stage for the establishment of the totalitarian state and a personal dictatorship is illustrated by the case of Ghana. Almost total suppression of personal liberty and the development of a "cult of personality," in which the adulation of Nkrumah surpasses in revolting phraseology the sycophancy of the regime of Stalin in Soviet Russia if it has not yet attained its bloodiness, now characterize the totalitarian state in Ghana. It is by no means clear, however, that the creation of a dictatorship has solved the most critical problems of capital saving and investment in that country.

III

In Latin America the conflict between socioeconomic reform and the accumulation of capital for industrialization has taken even more complex forms than in the underdeveloped countries of Africa and Asia. It is an article of faith among intellectuals in the United States that economic progress in Latin America depends upon economic reform. The credo further runs that economic reform is blocked by the political power of reactionary landlords and capitalists. By economic reform is meant, in the first instance, redistribution of wealth and income.

Criticism of this credo is difficult because in one sense or another most of it is true. Income classes at all levels in all countries resist the redistribution of wealth and income in favor of income receivers in lower brackets. Apparently Latin-American wealth-holders do resist the redistribution of income more strongly than in the United States and Western Europe, where redistribution through social security legislation and other means has come to be accepted as unavoidable, if not positively desirable. The contrast between luxurious living of the country-club type and the shanty slums of the cities is far sharper in Latin America than the difference between the styles of living of richer and poorer in the United States or in Western Europe. The Latin-American capitalist with the record of Castro before his eyes steps up his long-established custom of hedging against political uncertainties by investing abroad all the funds he can get through the foreign-exchange controls. This "flight capital" is augmented by the funds of politicians who have also learned to use this hedge against adverse turns of the wheel of fortune.

As for internal investment, the Latin-American capitalist naturally turns to more speculative investment with high returns and the shortest possible "pay-out period." These investment opportunities may be associated with governmental contracts and political corruption, as has been charged in Brazil, for example. In cases where the most extreme inequality in the ownership of land exists, as in Chile, the landlord is not likely to be inclined toward long-term investments to improve the productivity of his land when he is fighting off attempts to expropriate him.

The government of the United States, indeed, insists on most of these socioeconomic reforms as a prerequisite for extending economic aid under the Alliance for Progress. The position of the United States government is that unless the tax resources of the countries to be aided are fully exploited, it is unreasonable to expect American taxpayers to provide economic aid. This means that upper-income receivers in Latin-American countries should, through progressive tax rates, be required to pay as high rates of taxes as do those in the United States.

Since in many, if not in most, Latin-American countries, upper-income receivers do not pay nearly as large a proportion of their incomes in taxes as is true in the United States, it is easy to come to the conclusion that this undesirable state of affairs can be accounted for simply by the control of Latin-American governments by the reactionary upper classes. It is an easy step to the next conclusion: namely, that the remedy must be for conservative governments to be superseded by more liberal or radical governments. These more liberal or radical governments could then be expected to increase taxes on upper-bracket incomes, promote collective bargaining and higher payments to workers, carry out land reforms by distributing the large estates among small landowners, and in general reduce the inequality of wealth and income. No one wants this to be done by Communist-dominated parties or movements, of course. Indeed, it is generally maintained that carrying out such a policy of socioeconomic reform is the really effective way to prevent a Castro-Communist type of take-over in Latin America.

There can be no doubt that if rates of taxation on upper incomes were raised, if these taxes were actually collected, and if tax receipts were used to pay for more and better schools, road construction, and other productivity-promoting activities of government, an increased rate of economic growth would be promoted thereby. There can likewise be no doubt that, from a social standpoint, measures to decrease the inequality of distribution of wealth and income would be desirable if these could be taken without a net loss in productivity.

It is true that under the most favorable circumstances and the most effective administration, these socioeconomic reforms would even facilitate the capital formation essential to economic growth. Unfortunately, there can be no guarantee that the victory of a party with proclaimed radical goals will increase total tax receipts from upper-income groups, since measures to increase the wages of workers or to bring about redistribution of landholdings may limit or diminish production. The mistake of liberals in the United States is to assume that since redistribution of income in Latin America is desirable, almost any overt act in this direction, at least if it is not directly attributable to the Communists, will increase economic productivity.

In Chile, for example, the money wages of copper miners are already some four times the national industrial average. In addition, there are very substantial fringe benefits, including hospitalization on a lavish scale. In this case, increasing the wages of copper miners would certainly diminish investment in the copper industry and reduce the real income of other workers in Chile. Indeed, both the Anaconda and Kennecott copper companies have already cut back their investment programs drastically.

Likewise, land redistribution in Chile could be carried out without reducing production only on the basis of a most carefully administered and necessarily complex system. There can be no doubt that many large estates in Chile could be farmed just as efficiently or even more efficiently if they were no more than, say, one-fourth their present size. But suppose a large estate is divided up among, say, two or three hundred agricultural laborers. What then? Furthermore, if the *latifundia* are to be subdivided and redistributed, who is to obtain the land? The laborers on a particular estate, or the dwellers on the *minifundia*, perhaps in some distant area where the size of the holdings is far too small either for efficient farming or to furnish a family livelihood? It is not impossible to work out plans or to administer a land redistribution program in the face of these problems, as land redistribution in postwar Italy has demonstrated. It is difficult to do so without setting up an administrative bureaucracy that would absorb the rental values formerly going to the landlords, as the Italian experience also indicates.

Such difficulties need not and should not prevent carrying out programs of redistribution of wealth and income in Latin America. Legislation that would authorize a small beginning was passed in 1962 in Chile. A small beginning has actually been made in Columbia on the basis of legislation passed several years ago. It must be recognized that these reforms cannot be counted upon in their early stages to facilitate economic growth. The kind of financial reform necessary to prevent run-away inflation, whether due to "cost push" wage inflation, speculation, or simply to printing press inflation, is a very different kind of economic reform from that advocated by liberals in the United States and radical leaders in Latin America. Unfortunately, economic reform that simply involves measures intended to redistribute wealth and income and to make economic growth possible will often be in conflict, and it is vital that this be recognized.

President Betancourt has demonstrated in Venezuela that it is possible to devise an economic program in which measures for social reform and for economic growth can be made reasonably compatible. His experience demonstrates also the extremes to which Communists and rightists will go to frustrate such a program. This is likely to be true in the case of such programs in the other countries of Latin America as well.

Countries that are presently underdeveloped now have the opportunity to abridge drastically the time required by the countries of Europe to acquire both the techniques and the capital required for industrialization. Underdeveloped countries can now import the techniques of advanced industrial countries instead of having to develop the techniques themselves. This transfer of techniques is further very greatly facilitated by financial aid and technical assistance furnished gratis or at low rates by the already industrialized countries. None of the already industrialized countries had this special form of assistance from other countries.

There is also evidence that the ratio between population and natural resources is no longer so determinative in productivity as was formerly true. This development by no means eliminates the hazards of the "population explosion," but it does afford the possibility of developing economic viability if the rate of population increase can be kept within bounds.

Since in the industrialized countries of the West some 70 to 80 per cent of value added in production represents labor costs, if underdeveloped countries can keep wage rates down so that this percentage is smaller, they can become competitive on international markets. They must become internationally competitive if they are to be able to pay for imports of capital equipment and the most essential consumer goods. This is to say that in underdeveloped countries with high ratios of population to natural and capital resources, their chief resource is cheap labor. If labor costs per unit of product rise faster than labor productivity, this resource is dissipated.

The economic problems of underdeveloped countries, in restricting the power of the various economic groups and subgroups to seize more income for themselves than can be permitted if economic growth is to take place, differ only in degree and in detail from those of the industrially more advanced countries such as the United States, the United Kingdom, and France. In these countries problems of restricting inflation, securing adequate rates of economic growth, preventing unacceptable levels of unemployment and the like also turn on the still unsolved problems of how to limit or control the economic and political power of particular economic groups. This involves finding supplements to or a partial substitute for the free market that used to perform this function. One could wish nostalgically that the restoration of the free market could be recommended both to developed and underdeveloped countries as the sovereign solution for these problems. The retention of as much of the free-market mechanism as possible is still to be recommended. However, the phrase "as much as possible" identifies this recommendation for what it is, an attitude and not a program.

While the underdeveloped countries are struggling with these problems, it is essential that the task of their governments should not be made more difficult by our promoting the revolution of rising expectations or pretending that socioeconomic reforms always promote economic growth.

IMPLICATIONS OF ECONOMIC
DEVELOPMENT

*Sayre P. Schatz**

Most of the world is engaged in a strenuous, even frantic, struggle for economic development. The fate of governments often depends upon their success in this effort, and the stature of nations and peoples is judged by the degree of economic wealth they have achieved.

In this essay we step back and examine some of the wider implications of economic development. What is the point of economic development? Why should we foster it? For what ends or purposes? What social changes are bound up with economic growth? In order to make themselves capable of sustaining economic growth it is widely believed that most of the economically less developed societies must transform themselves in fundamental ways. These basic changes are conceived of as the social *preconditions* of economic growth; the social *consequences* may also be profound. The pattern and tempo of modern economic activity and the alleviation of poverty will profoundly affect established values and modes of behavior.

The policy implications of economic development are also serious. Development is a difficult process. (If it were not, the problem of national poverty would be fading into oblivion.)

* The author wishes to thank Gerald Helleiner, of the Nigerian Institute of Social and Economic Research and the Yale University Economic Growth Center, and Peter Lloyd, of the University of Ibadan, Nigeria, for their helpful comments.

Economic growth calls for a head-on confrontation with intractable economic problems. It requires painful changes in established ways of life and the adoption of measures that arouse the antagonism of vested interests and classes. A satisfactory rate of development therefore requires bold policies and calculated leaps into the dark.

Some of economic development's implications for policy will be touched upon in this essay. We in the West have generally been afraid to encourage new approaches and have stuck with staid, comfortably familiar policies that have shown themselves to be inadequate. We have been fearful of fundamental change. "We have preferred to let foreign economic development lag, rather than to stir up the brew of social upheaval."[1] In the opinion of this writer a bolder outlook on the part of the West is called for.

I. *The Ends of Development*

It can be persuasively argued that the pursuit of well-being through economic development is a chimera, that the disruption, envy, frustration and anguish brought on by economic development at least match the benefits it brings. It is therefore pertinent to inquire into the *ends* of economic development. Paraphrasing the vulgar expression "What's in it for me?" we may ask, "What's in it for mankind?"

Economists have been wrestling with this topic, off and on, for hundreds of years. Let us consider what has been said about this in three major streams of economic thought: the classical, as represented by Adam Smith; the revolutionary, as represented by Karl Marx; and the variegated contemporary stream of development economics.

For Adam Smith the ends and the process of development

1. Robert L. Heilbroner, *The Future as History* (New York, 1960), p. 165. This book is a most stimulating discussion of the historic currents of our time.

are inextricably related. The end of development is, in a sense, the free unrolling of the process of development. We therefore consider briefly Smith's theory of this process. In his view society is a developing organism and his purpose is to explain what makes it evolve and where it is going.[2] The basic dynamic force in society's development according to Smith is the accumulation of capital, which results from a powerful drive of the capitalist class for material well-being and prestige. The accumulation of capital, in the form of growing productive facilities, brings about an increasing demand for labor, and hence rising wages. Profits tend to fall as a result, and the incentive for capital accumulation lags. If this tendency were to continue unchecked, society would soon stagnate. However, in Smith's theory the rise in wage rates soon leads, primarily through a reduction in the appalling childhood-mortality rate, to an expansion in population. Because of the early age at which children start working, this is rapidly translated into an enlarged supply of labor. Wages are therefore prevented from rising too much or are pushed down again. Profit is thereby safeguarded, and thus capital accumulation and economic development can proceed further.

This development may seem circular, but until an ultimate "stationary state" is reached, it is really a spiral process. The continuously accumulated capital is embodied not simply in an increasing *mass* of productive facilities; these facilities are *technically improved*. Production *per capita* consequently increases. This defeats the tendency of population growth to drive wages all the way back to the original level. At each turn of the spiral of development, the basic wage level (the "natural wage") tends to rise.

For Adam Smith, the *end* of economic development was the

2. In my discussion of Adam Smith, I am greatly indebted to the excellent article by Adolph Lowe, "The Classical Theory of Economic Growth," *Social Research*, XXI (Summer, 1954), 127-158.

unfolding of this process of development. The improvement in the level of living of the vast majority, which he viewed as unquestionably desirable, was a manifestation of the social harmony inherent in the Providential natural order. The harmonious process of economic change was guided as by an invisible hand. Laissez faire was championed by Smith as a means of sweeping away the man-made impediments to this process, so that natural development, which Smith passionately desired, could be realized. As Lionel Robbins has said: "The System of Economic Freedom was not just a detached recommendation not to interfere: It was an urgent demand that what were thought to be hampering and anti-social impediments should be removed and that the immense potential of free pioneering individual initiative should be released."[3]

Karl Marx, like Adam Smith, was concerned with the nature and destination of a process of economic development that pushed forward inexorably. The *end* for Marx may be said to be socialism; the basic motive force is technological progress. This force powers an impressive process of capitalist development and drives society on to socialism.

Technological progress renders existing methods of production obsolete. Capitalists therefore must adopt new methods of production if their businesses are to survive. The new techniques use more capital per worker, however; capitalists are therefore *forced* to accumulate capital. They also *desire* to invest in improved productive equipment, for those who pioneer in this way reap extra profits until their rivals catch up.

Capital accumulation and technological progress, which are the essence of capitalist development, have a number of profound effects. Technological advance creates a reserve army of unemployed because modern large-scale equipment tends to be labor-displacing. The demand for labor therefore lags

3. Lionel Robbins, *The Theory of Economic Policy in English Classical Political Economy* (London, 1952), p. 19.

behind the growth of population, and an increasing pool of unemployment is created. A highly important consequence of capitalist development, as Marx sees it, is a series of ever-worsening depressions. Although technological progress brings a rapid rise in production, consumption in a capitalist society is limited. The competitive struggle forces the capitalist to expropriate an ever-increasing portion of the value the workers create. The worker is therefore unable to provide a substantial enough market for the things he produces, while the capitalist's consumption is limited by his need and desire to devote his income to capital accumulation.

These and other irrationalities of capitalism engender among the working class a powerful desire to replace capitalism. At the same time, the objective conditions necessary for the establishment of socialism have been created: the economy has become a huge, interdependent productive mechanism, and a disciplined working class accustomed to working together has emerged. Capitalism is discarded; "the expropriators are expropriated."

The end of economic development for Marx, as for Smith, is the full unfolding of an immanent process of economic development. For Adam Smith the system extant was the desirable one; only the impediments to its beneficent unrolling were to be removed. For Marx, however, the capitalist system itself had become an impediment; the unfolding of the development process involved a *destination*, the socialist stage of human development. In a socialist society, as Marx views it, man at last leaves behind his prehistory, when he is subject to the often malignant influences of social forces beyond his comprehension and control, when "society is an immense stamping press for the careless production of underdeveloped and malformed human beings, and . . . is not . . . fundamentally concerned with moral issues, with serious purposes, or with human dignity."[4] True human history begins; man uses

4. Heilbroner, *op. cit.*, p. 199.

his intelligence to shape society in a rational and humane way. There is a fuller, freer development of the individual. A better and more fulfilled human race comes into being.

When we come to contemporary development economics, the left, center, and right all affirm the desirability of economic growth. The nature of this affirmation is flavored by the political leanings of the writer. P. T. Bauer and Basil Yamey, who may be called philosophical descendants of Adam Smith (preferring as close an approximation to laissez faire as possible), link their description of the ends of economic growth with the position that the state should play a limited role and that "it is for the members of society to choose among the alternative opportunities open to them and develop them with the aid of their personal endowments and the property they own."[5] On the other side, the left, identifying with the underdog, who is most obviously affected by economic backwardness, tends to feel that the desirability of economic advance is self-evident, and may charge that skepticism on this score objectively serves reactionary ends. According to Paul Baran, an accomplished Marxist economist, the skeptic often "denies the possibility of a rational judgment on the usefulness, let alone urgency, of economic and social change in colonial and dependent areas, and counsels utmost caution in disturbing the continuity of the backward societies." Such an approach "supplies aid and comfort not to the peoples in the colonial and dependent countries struggling for [economic] freedom but to their masters seeking to preserve the *status quo*."[6] The center, always concerned about seeing both sides of the question, tempers its enthusiasm for economic growth by reflections on the social disruption caused by economic development, the meanness of spirit that might accompany concentration on economic gains and losses, the minimization

5. Peter T. Bauer and Basil S. Yamey, *The Economics of Under-developed Countries* (Chicago, 1957), p. 149.
6. Paul A. Baran, *The Political Economy of Growth* (New York, 1957), p. 17.

of man in the face of the huge organizations that he himself creates as a part of economic growth, and other problems.

Still, virtually all agree on the desirability of economic growth. W. Arthur Lewis, who has written the most systematic and extensive contemporary discussion of the ends of economic development and whose thought is representative of the best in contemporary mainstream economics, puts it this way: "The advantage of economic growth is not that wealth increases happiness, but that it increases the range of human choice." Economic development, by augmenting the supply of the essentials of life, enables us to choose life rather than death; i.e., it enables more children to live out their lives and it extends man's life span; it allows us to choose greater leisure; it permits us to choose more goods and more services; it particularly benefits women who in most economically underdeveloped societies are little more than beasts of burden; it allows us to choose "the luxury of greater humanitarianism."[7]

Contemporary economics reinforces its belief in the desirability of economic development with an argument about its necessity. As Lewis puts it, "two developments . . . make it imperative not to retard but to accelerate further growth. One of these is the fact that aspirations have grown faster than production. And the other is the fact that death rates are falling faster than birth rates."[8] The people in the underdeveloped economies have seen how the rich sector of the world lives, and they are determined to move toward that level of living. Moreover, the rising population makes increasing production imperative even if the level of living is only to stand still. Arguments about whether greater affluence has made or will make men happier or better are beside the point. The point is that things will surely get worse if economic development does not proceed apace.

7. W. Arthur Lewis, *The Theory of Economic Growth* (Homewood, Illinois, 1955), p. 420.
8. *Ibid.*, p. 434.

Three beliefs concerning the ends of development emerge from this brief survey. First, virtually all strands of economics express the belief, or perhaps only the faith, that greater economic well-being is associated with greater human welfare. I share this conviction. True, there are disruptions and strains. But it is easy for the affluent to lose sight of the misery attending poverty. To mention just one facet of this misery, a pediatrician working in Nigeria estimates that about half of the children die before reaching the age of ten.[9] Another pediatrician, who returned from the hospital looking particularly haggard one day a week, explained upon questioning that this was the day he had to "play God." He had to decide just which of the large number of waiting children to admit to the hospital and which ones to turn away in the full knowledge that many of the latter would surely die. Second, moving from desirability to necessity, modern economists stress, correctly I believe, the malignant consequences for the world of a failure to develop. Finally, the great economists of the classical period, such as Adam Smith and Karl Marx, particularly stress a long view of the human condition. Economic growth is part of a grand development process that will produce a better kind of society and therefore a better kind of human being. In any case, the choice is not up to the people of the wealthier economies. The people of the poor countries passionately desire economic growth and by one means or another they will have it.

II. *The Impact of Economic Change on Traditional Patterns*

Leaving aside questions about the desirability of economic development and assuming that it is going to take place, let us turn to another issue: the desirability of preserving, despite the tumultuous nature of the process of development, traditional values and modes of behavior that are important to the

9. Robert Collis, *An African Encounter* (New York, 1960), p. 93.

people of the developing countries. Discussion of this topic has looked in two directions, to the social conditions that may need to precede economic development, and to the social changes that may be consequences of economic development. In reverse order, the social *consequences* of economic advance are dealt with in this section and the social *preconditions* in the following one.

It is no longer necessary to emphasize, as it once was, that the people of the poor countries are not "lesser breeds without the law," that their patterns of human relationship, their patterns of culture may be worth cherishing. It is my belief, nevertheless, that much of the concern expressed on this issue is academic and futile, and to the extent that overconcern with preserving the old culture directs attention away from the more important need to influence in a salutary manner the implantation of the new ways, such concern may even be positively harmful.

A fundamental social transformation is underway in the less developed countries. This transformation is profound, it is rapid, and it is inevitable.

The extent of the social change wrought by economic development and the historical rapidity of contemporary social change may be suggested by two examples, one from Medieval Europe and the other from present day Africa.

An economically propelled transformation in deeply held social values, embodied in and reinforced by religious doctrine, is illustrated by the changes during the Middle Ages in the practice of charging interest on loans and in the corresponding doctrine of usury. Church doctrine in the early Middle Ages condemned interest; regardless of the rate or the circumstances the exaction of interest was "usury" and was considered an unjust practice. This condemnation was not surprising in the light of prevailing economic conditions. Profitable investment of money in a modern sense was practically nonexistent and loans were generally made to persons who needed the money because of some exigency. Charging interest was therefore seen as a nasty and uncharitable act. The usurer was taking advantage of a person in trouble.

As commerce developed during the later Middle Ages, however, the practice of borrowing money for profitable investment spread. The earlier social and economic basis for the condemnation of usury thus crumbled; the borrower raised money not because of personal difficulties but for economic gain. The lender naturally insisted on sharing in the gain, and the practice of levying interest developed inexorably. Corresponding roughly with the change in practice there was a slow piecemeal change in values and religious doctrines.[10] Step by step concessions were made. Concession: if a loss were suffered by the lender as a consequence of making the loan, he was justified in taking interest. Concession: when repayment was delayed, the lender had a right to compensate himself for the inconvenience caused by exacting a penalty in the nature of interest; gradually the length of the period after which the "penalty" could be exacted was shortened until, later, it practically disappeared altogether. Concession (a most significant one): if the lender lost the chance of gain because of his loan, charging interest was justified. Concession: if the lender undertook any risk, interest was justified as a reward for this risk. Thus, bit by bit, over the centuries, an unquestioned value, the attitude toward interest, reversed itself.

The incomparably more rapid social transformation being brought about in this era by economic development may be illustrated by the alterations in African practices and doctrines concerning land tenure.

Land has been essentially a corporate possession in African societies, belonging to family, lineage, or village groups. The community rather than the individual has had the basic rights over the land, which was apportioned by the chief or other proper community authorities. In the more settled com-

10. This was not a simple chronological process, and the account here is oversimplified.

munities, families or individuals have generally had permanent (though qualified) rights to this land so long as it was worked to satisfy their needs. When they stopped using the land, it reverted to the community and could be redistributed to others who needed it. This communal or co-operative system of landholding harmonized with the economic situation; pastoral activities and rotational cultivation (in which a patch of land is cleared, the land is farmed for a few years, and then is "bush" fallowed for a number of years while the cultivator goes on to another piece of land) have both been carried out in a communal or co-operative manner.

Although the traditional system of landholding is of central importance in most African cultures, the system is changing with incredible rapidity under the impact of economic opportunity and necessity. "In almost every area in which subsistence cultivation has given place to the cultivation of marketable crops there can now be found instances of the commercialization of land rights," Lord Hailey said in 1956. "Hitherto the modifications made in traditional procedure have followed, as it were automatically, on changes in economic circumstances, but it is probable that the process will now be definitely stimulated by measures taken to implement official policy."[11] As one surveys changes in land tenure throughout Africa, a correlation becomes evident between the degree of economic development and the degree of departure from traditional landholding patterns. In some parts of Ghana, e.g., in those in which cocoa proved to be a most lucrative crop, commercialization of land proceeded so rapidly that it was already said in 1931 that the traditional landholding system was virtually destroyed.[12]

Several major steps can be delineated, as I see it, in the development of practices regarding alienation of land.[13]

First, there is *minor modification* of the traditional land-

11. Lord Hailey, *An African Survey* (London, 1957), p. 803.
12. *Ibid.*, p. 793.
13. It may not be necessary to remark that what follows is an oversimplified, somewhat idealized scheme.

holding pattern in order to accommodate capitalistic economic drives. Traditional corporate ownership still prevails,
but the rules are stretched here and there. For example, where
tobacco growing has proved profitable in Nyasaland, some
African tobacco growers have enlarged their landholdings by
applying in the traditional manner to the chiefs. While these
tobacco growers have not claimed the right to dispose of the
additional land, they have nevertheless resisted, sometimes
successfully, a few attempts by the chiefs to reallot this land
to fellow tribesmen who needed it. This resistance illustrates,
incidentally, a common pattern of change: formal recognition
of old laws or customs accompanied by disregard of them in
practice.

The next stage is *quasi-purchase* of land, by which is meant
land acquisition in a way that approximates individual purchase, though it is not legally recognized as such. Permanent
transfers which in practice amount to sales have become common in Kano Province of Nigeria, e.g., although they are not
legally recognized in that the Emir and his Council insist
that land cannot be sold. This kind of permanent transfer has
become increasingly common in many parts of Africa. In these
cases, a high degree of individual control over the land usually develops although community controls are not completely
absent. Quasi-purchase also occurs through modifications in
various traditional practices, such as pledging of land. In
pledging, money is advanced to the holder of land who in
return transfers the right to use the land to the lender until
the loan is repaid. The practice of pledging admits of many
variations, but many types of pledge "now closely approach
the English concept of mortgage, though in a much simpler
form."[14] Pledging is often done on such terms now that re-
demption of the land by the "borrower" is quite difficult, and

14. Peter C. Lloyd, *Yoruba Land Law* (published for the Nigerian Institute
of Social and Economic Research by the Oxford University Press: London,
1962), p. 309. There is much interesting material on pawning as well as
pledging in chap. x of this definitive study of Yoruba landholding practices.

the transaction is practically equivalent to sale of the pledged land.

The third stage may be called *impeded purchase*. Legal purchase of land for economic uses occurs, but it is hampered by customs or by laws derived from these customs which restrict the terms of the transaction. Thus the kind of purchaser may be circumscribed. Among the Kamba of Kenya, e.g., the holder of land may have a full right to sell, but only to a member of his tribe. In some areas there is greater latitude; any African purchaser is acceptable; only non-African purchasers are proscribed. The conditions under which sales are made may also be restricted. Sales of land are considered permissible among some Kikuyus, for example, but only with the consent of all members of the community. The nature of the restrictions varies greatly from area to area.

Finally, there is *free purchase* of land. Even within this category, there are various shadings of control, and traditional carryovers involving some restrictions on the use and disposal of land are common. This stage has been reached in many places in Africa, particularly in the cities.

Transformations from traditional to capitalistic ways are also taking place in other landholding practices. In the renting or leasing of land, e.g., the traditional ceremonial offering to the holder of permanent rights is being replaced by modern monetary rent. Many other changes of this nature are occurring, but there is insufficient space to describe them.

These changes in landholding practices are of fundamental importance, for the land has had deep emotional meaning for Africans. It has not only been the chief source of livelihood; it has also been interwoven into social and religious beliefs and practices. It has often been at the very center of the society, and Africans have been extremely sensitive about any attempts to change their relationship with their land. As Lord Hailey has said, speaking of land policy in Africa: "There is certainly no one feature of Colonial policy which has had an equal influence in determining the character of the relations between the indigenous people and a Colonial Administration."[15] The fiercest resistance to colonial rule often arose in response to land policies.

Thus, just as the fact that money could be increasingly used as a means of earning more money led to the breakdown of the medieval values and practices regarding the collection of interest, similarly, the fact that land has become an increasingly important means of earning money has led to the breakdown of the traditional values and practices concerning land. While the former transformation took centuries, however, the latter—which involves a profound and fundamental alteration in the entire society—is taking only decades. Modern economic development causes swift and fundamental social change.

III. *Preconditions of Economic Development*

It is widely suggested that economic development must also be *preceded* by basic social change. Current thinking about preconditions of economic development has been powerfully influenced by W. W. Rostow's popular book on stages of economic growth.[16] In order to achieve a self-sustaining process of economic development, according to Rostow's thesis, a nation must first go through a period of "slow moving changes" during which it painfully creates the preconditions for economic growth. A profound political, social and technological transformation must be wrought before the society can respond to economic stimuli in a positive, self-reinforcing way. The society must develop men who are capable of manipulating and applying modern science; it must develop imaginative, daring, and efficient entrepreneurs; a class of people

---

15. Hailey, *op. cit.*, p. 686. The discussion of land tenure in the essay relies heavily on this basic work.

16. W. W. Rostow, *The Stages of Economic Growth* (Cambridge, 1960).

must emerge who are willing to entrust money to the entrepreneurs; roads, harbors, supplies of electricity and many other forms of overhead capital must be created; a new elite which regards modernization as desirable and possible must come into power; the horizon of expectations must rise; proper political conditions must be created, and many other changes must occur.

The achievement of the preconditions is a slow process. Their attainment, says a United States Senate study on economic growth, "requires the passage of time; time for the social structure to be altered; time for new political attitudes and institutions to be created and consolidated; time for the creation of the skills and habits and institutions on which capital formation depends. Above all, time must pass for new generations to succeed one another, each finding the environment, techniques, and goals of modernization a bit more familiar and acceptable."[17]

Rostow presents his preconditions thesis as a generalization valid for all types of societies, but in fact its applicability depends upon the orientation of investment in the "directly productive sector" of the economy. ("Directly productive" investments are the industrial, commercial and agricultural activities which, in a private-enterprise economy, are normally the sphere of business concerns. These are distinguished from the supporting "overhead capital" investments—roads, port facilities, railroads, other public utilities—which in most of the world are generally provided by government.) If an underdeveloped country restricts itself to profit-seeking investment in the directly productive sphere, then it is true that the country cannot have a high rate of investment and thus a high rate of economic growth unless the preconditions exist.

17. United States Senate, Committee on Foreign Relations, *Economic Social and Political Change in Underdeveloped Countries and Its Implications for United States Policy*, Study No. 12, prepared by the Center for International Studies, Massachusetts Institute of Technology, 86th Congress, 22nd Session (1960), p. 21.

"There's nothing so shy as a million dollars." Without congenial social, technological, and political conditions, profit is uncertain and therefore investment and economic growth are likely to be limited.

However, the preconditions thesis need not be valid in economies where considerations of monetary profitability do not hold full sway over investment in the directly productive sector. A high rate of economically useful rather than pecuniarily profitable investment in this sector and therefore in the economy as a whole need not await the prior creation of preconditions. This point rests on the difference between the pecuniary profitability and the economic utility of investment, which must be explained at some length.

Investment in the directly productive sector need not yield a *monetary* profit, i.e., a net return to business, in order to yield an *economic* profit, i.e., a net benefit to the economy. Investments generate many benefits for a less developed economy that are not reflected in the monetary calculation of profit and loss, so that the economic utility of new investments often far exceeds pecuniary profitability. This is especially true since the less developed countries usually assign a high national priority to economic development, and consequently prize, as necessary for development, social changes that would otherwise be considered disruptive.

The divergencies between economic profitability and business profitability take many forms, a few of which will be illustrated here.

1. Perhaps the most important example of this divergence occurs when enterprises are established that utilize productive resources that would otherwise be idle. This increases a country's production (real income) regardless of the monetary profitability of the undertaking. There is abundant opportunity for such production in Nigeria; this will be discussed in Section IV.

2. An immensely important economic benefit accruing from the development of new enterprises, and only partially

realized in the investor's money return, is the labor skill thereby created. Experience is the best teacher. Labor becomes skilled, disciplined, accustomed to the routine and regularity characteristic of modern productive processes, and responsible in handling expensive equipment to the degree that it learns these attributes through experience. Two of the largest indigenously owned enterprises in Nigeria—a tire retreading firm and a business engaged in many activities, including contracting, furniture production, and road transport—hire, for the most part, unskilled and untrained labor. These enterprises nevertheless function successfully because their workers have acquired the requisite skills through on-the-job training and experience. Most countries undertake large expenditures for vocational and technical education; the same sort of social benefit is created by experience in productive enterprises.

Conversely, the absence of experience perpetuates the inaptitude of labor. This in turn tarnishes profit prospects, and a vicious circle is completed because this prevents the establishment of new, skill-creating enterprises. An investigation into hurricane lamp production in Nigeria by the United Africa Company illustrates the drag caused by lack of experience. The assembly of hurricane lamps in Nigeria seemed promising; the market has been a substantial one, more than a million lamps being imported annually, and there were several other propitious conditions. The decision, however, was against assembly in Nigeria. The chief reason was lack of certain experience-created labor skills. "In the United Kingdom factory skill based on years of experience is the key factor. . . ." Since Nigeria lacked industrial experience, the necessary skills could have been provided only by expensive expatriate personnel or by a long, costly on-the-job training program in Britain.[18]

3. Invaluable managerial and entrepreneurial skills are

18. "Industrialization in West Africa," *Statistical and Economic Review* (United Africa Company) , No. 23 (Sept., 1959) , pp. 19-21.

also created primarily by experience. The road transport business in Nigeria provides a good illustration. Although a truck is a large, complex piece of equipment, the business is a relatively simple one and people with little prior knowledge of modern business practices have been able to enter successfully. One of the important benefits created by entry of Nigerians into this business has been the development of a group of modern Nigerian entrepreneurs. A student of business enterprise in Nigeria found that these men have ventured further; the Nigerians associated with the beginnings of light industry are largely those who have been successful in road transport.[19]

4. Production in the directly productive sector also yields other economic returns not reflected in the monetary returns of the producing unit. The establishment of new producing units encourages production of various intermediate goods and services. The commencement of cigarette manufacturing in Nigeria, e.g., enlarged the market for tobacco and thereby induced an expansion in the production of that crop. Income generated by new enterprises expands the markets of existing firms and may make possible larger scale and more efficient techniques of production. By entering fields that have been monopolistically controlled, new undertakings may curtail monopolistic practices.

Thus many benefits not reflected in profits are generated by investment in new enterprises. Conventional economic policies grossly underrate the importance of divergencies between economic and pecuniary profitability. The fact that all economists warmly support investments which meet the profitability criterion constitutes, it seems to me, implicit support for the position that benefits from the undertaking of new factories or other enterprises may far exceed the money profit.

19. E. K. Hawkins, *Road Transport in Nigeria* (published for the Nigerian Institute of Social and Economic Research by Oxford University Press: London, 1958), p. 94.

If profit *did* represent all or almost all the net social gain from the establishment of an enterprise, then the gain would accrue in the first instance solely to the profit recipient; if he in turn transferred all his profits abroad, the nation presumably would not benefit at all. The vying for new enterprises by less developed countries, or for that matter by localities and depressed areas in prosperous nations, would then make little sense. But it is virtually universally agreed that seeking new enterprises does make sense, that new investments are (apart from the use of the profits) vitally important for developing economies. Such accordance is really nothing less than agreement that the net economic benefits of investment beyond those represented by profit are substantial.

If my argument is correct—that there are many economically productive investment opportunities which are not monetarily profitable—then it follows that it is *possible* for a country to have a high rate of economically useful investment in the directly productive sector without awaiting the prior creation of Rostow's preconditions. While these conditions—the growth promoting attitudes, patterns of behavior, skills, and kinds of people—must already exist for large amounts of investment to be profitable, it is not necessary that they exist beforehand for large amounts of investment to be economically useful. As a matter of fact, one of the far-reaching benefits of investment is that it *creates* the so-called preconditions. Capital formation and the other conditions required for substantial economic growth are interrelated and mutually reinforcing. The accumulation of modern capital is probably the quickest and most efficacious way of *developing* the experience, the skill, the acclimatization to modern economic processes, and the other social conditions necessary for rapid economic growth. In other words, the preconditions of a high rate of investment are really *coconditions*, created by and simultaneously with the investment.

I have argued that a high rate of economically productive

investment is possible without awaiting the prior establishment of preconditions—if a country discards the oversimplified orthodoxy that equates private profitability and net
economic usefulness. This does not mean that a sustained high
rate of investment is easy to achieve. There are many grave
problems which it would be foolish to overlook or minimize.
What it does mean is that the orientation needed for solving
these problems should be broadened, that policies confined
within the narrow bounds of the old comfortable orthodoxies
are incapable of handling the vast problems of economic development. One way in which the broader outlook suggested
here may be helpful is suggested in the following section.

IV. *Orientation for Economic Development*

A feeling that doctrinaire reliance on monetary profitability hinders development provides one foundation of the
belief widely held in the poor countries that government must
take an active part in the economy. People in these countries
usually favor a mixed economy. They want the speedier development that appears to be associated with the more Com-
munist-oriented countries along with the relatively greater
freedom that appears to be associated with most of the more
advanced capitalist countries.

This best of both worlds combination may not be possible.
There are reasons for believing that rapid economic development may require an authoritarian government. Mobilization
of a nation's will and energy, imposition of higher taxes,
actions that interfere with old ways and with the privileges
of powerful groups—all of these require a strong government.
Still the possibility of a union of rapid development and a
fair measure of political and civil freedom cannot be ruled
out. This combination might be achieved, I believe, if the
less developed economies were to undertake imaginative and
strenuous efforts to make relatively full use of the underutilized productive capacity with which they abound.

One is struck in most underdeveloped economies by the extent of the underutilized productive resources of all kinds. There is an abundance of labor seeking jobs. Rural labor is frequently underemployed or seasonally unemployed. Many laborers "do not work as many hours in the year as they could easily do." In particular, there are "months of almost complete idleness experienced by many farmers during the dry season."[20] Underemployment and open unemployment also abound in the cities. When the manager of a tobacco factory in Nigeria, e.g., was asked whether he could expand his labor force without raising wages, he replied that "his only problem would be to control the mob of applicants."[21] Jobs are so precious that in West Africa, for example, a person who can control or influence the choice of an applicant can sell his influence for as much as a month's wages. A widespread "confidence game" in the sale of nonexistent jobs has developed. This fraudulent practice has become so common that the government of Ghana has felt it necessary publicly to threaten stern action against such swindlers. In Northern Nigeria, the government has appointed a committee to study the problem of corruption in the obtaining of employment and to advise on means to eliminate it.[22]

In some countries there are also vast areas of idle arable land. The leading agricultural economist in Nigeria estimates that more than half of Nigeria's *cultivable* land is idle. This does *not* include the large areas in bush fallow, i.e., land which is part of the agricultural system but which is being left temporarily idle while it regains its fertility.[23] There is also a great deal of only partially utilized capital. Most indigenous enterprises are capable of sharply expanding their output, even doubling or tripling it, if they simply were to utilize their existing productive capacity to the full. It is quite

20. G. Brian Stapleton, *The Wealth of Nigeria* (London, 1958), pp. 61, 101.
21. P. T. Bauer, *West African Trade* (Cambridge, 1954), pp. 18-19.
22. *West Africa*, June 23, 1962, pp. 673, 692.
23. H. A. Oluwasanmi, "Agriculture in a Developing Economy: A Case Study in Nigerian Economic Development," unpublished manuscript, pp. 112, 116, 348.

ordinary for one to see the workers standing by idly in such enterprises simply because the firm has no orders for its output.

A tremendous boost to the development effort would be provided if some way could be found of activating this idle productive capacity—particularly in the production of capital goods, or in the production of export products or import substitutes, both of which would make more foreign exchange available for the purchase of capital goods. It seems to me that the chief reason for rapid economic growth in the Soviet Union, during its early plan years particularly, was not the efficacy of the planning, not the matching of input requirements with input availabilities, but the creation of an economic environment in which all output was desired, in which production was limited only by the ability to produce economically useful goods and never by the narrowness of the market. There existed, in essence, a condition of virtually unlimited demand. Output from existing productive capacity was therefore at a maximum. A powerful impetus was also provided to the rapid enlargement of that capacity.

The question that remains is whether the idle productive capacity can be set to work at economically useful activities without an excessive degree of regimentation. This question is related to Section III's discussion of the divergence between pecuniary and economic profitability. Although economically it would be immensely useful to set these underutilized productive factors to work, this will not happen without conscious direction of some kind. The conditions in the less developed economies are such that use of these factors of production would not be monetarily profitable.

Advanced economies have been confronted by a somewhat similar problem. Insufficient aggregate demand has depressed aggregate production by making it unprofitable. The accepted ("Keynesian") policy calls for government actions to increase aggregate expenditure beyond the "natural" level. Such policies are also helpful to some degree in the less developed economies. However, for reasons which cannot be gone into here, economists generally agree that Keynesian policies in these countries will still leave most of the underutilized productive capacity idle and that any substantial creation of aggregate demand will cause inflation. What is needed in the less developed economies, I believe, is demand creation for *individual* commodities comparable to Keynesian demand creation in the aggregate. Perhaps an effective approach, which I have suggested elsewhere,[24] may be the employment of what can be called "directed demand."

This approach calls for government to spend its own funds for (i.e., to direct government demand toward) particular commodities which have a net economic utility but which are nevertheless going unproduced because lack of "natural" demand makes their production unprofitable. The government would then sell these commodities at home or, in the case of export crops, abroad at a market clearing price, i.e., at a price low enough to induce potential purchasers to buy what was produced. For example, in Nigeria, many furniture producers are using only a limited portion of their productive capacity. The government could induce a great expansion in production by offering a set price to these firms for standard quality wooden furniture of certain kinds. This furniture could then be sold at market clearing prices to furnishers of homes and offices—who have been buying substantial quantities of imported furniture. The country would therefore save precious foreign exchange which could be used to pay for capital goods and expert services sorely needed for development. Idle resources would have been used to produce useful goods. National production and therefore national income would increase. The country would develop more rapidly.

24. "Underutilized Resources, 'Directed Demand,' and Deficit Financing: Illustrated by Reference to Nigeria," *Quarterly Journal of Economics,* LXXIII (Nov., 1959), 633-644.

The government would lose money on such a program, it is true. But the government outlays would flow into the national economy, augmenting monetary national income. The government could therefore finance this program without resort to inflation by increasing taxes on the increased level of national income. Since production would increase, an expanded money supply would be needed, so only part of the government expenditures on directed demand would need to be financed by taxation. Despite the higher level of taxes, the population's real and money income would be higher.

There may be other ways. Whatever the method, it is my conviction that a good part of the solution to the problem of rapid economic development lies in finding some way to make full use of the productive capacity lying idle in underdeveloped countries.

In summary, I have argued that economic development is desirable. I have maintained further that fortunately or unfortunately the social *consequences* of economic development will be profound, but that the belief that substantial social *preconditions* are necessary for a high level of investment is based on an oversimplified view of what constitutes useful investment, a view inapplicable to underdeveloped economies. I have therefore suggested that bolder policies are needed to meet the problems of development in poor countries, particularly to make use of their idle productive capacity. Finally, I took the liberty of advancing a particular policy proposal of my own, directed demand, which I think might activate the idle capacity in the less developed countries and thereby invigorate their process of development.

THE AFRICAN CONCEPTION OF
THE RULE OF LAW

Antony Allott

Is there an "African" conception of the Rule of Law? Is there justification for departures by modern African governments from the principles of the Rule of Law as generally accepted in Western countries? Can such justification be found, either in the institutions of law and government and the attitudes which inspire them, existing or formerly existing in traditional African societies, or in the special circumstances of contemporary Africa? These are some of the questions to which an answer will be sought in the present paper. It is hoped to discover how far the notions of the Rule of Law are rooted in the legal and governmental institutions of traditional Africa; but, before this task can be carried out, some preliminary questions must be considered and certain preliminary definitions attempted. In particular one must ask: what is the content of the so-called Rule of Law; and what sorts of societies existed, and on what basis was their public life organized in traditional Africa? In answering the latter question, we shall, of course, have to define "Africa" for the purposes of the present inquiry.

Once these preliminary questions have been cleared out of the way, an attempt will be made to examine: the concept of law in African societies; the relations of the executive to the law and to the people subject to the law; the notion of separation of powers; the law-making and adjudicating powers in

African society; whether the concept of fundamental or in-alienable rights paramount to man-made laws is to be found in traditional Africa; and finally, how far these principles, attitudes, beliefs, and institutions (in so far as we have been able to isolate and describe them) are relevant or accepted in the contemporary government of African peoples.

I. *The Societies of Traditional Africa*

Although the practice of dividing Africa into Africa north and south of the Sahara, respectively, is now falling out of favor—in sympathy with the continental and Pan-African approach to African problems—this division is both valid and convenient for the present inquiry. The profound difference in religion and patterns of government between the Islamic North and the pagan South would of itself suffice to justify separate consideration of the two halves of the continent, but ethnic differences are also relevant here. Accordingly, this paper will be restricted to conditions existing in Negro or tropical Africa south of the Sahara.

No one with the slightest acquaintance with traditional African systems of government would fall into the error of thinking that these systems were in any significant sense uniform, either in their structure or their functions,[1] since such systems range all the way from the tiny units of the Bushmen or the pigmies of the Ituri Forest,[2] who doubtfully have any formalized system of government at all, to the larger kin-based groupings of, say, the Kikuyu[3] or the Nuer,[4] and to the still

1. For a further consideration of African political systems and their classification see M. Fortes and E. E. Evans-Pritchard, eds., *African Political Systems* (1940); I. Schapera, *Government and Politics in Tribal Societies* (1956); J. Middleton and D. Tait, eds., *Tribes Without Rulers* (1958); L. Mair, *Primitive Government* (1962).
2. Described by C. Turnbull, *The Forest People* (1961) [Pigmies]; L. Marshall, "Kung Bushman Bands," *Africa* (1960), p. 325.
3. See H. E. Lambert, *Kikuyu Social and Political Institutions* (1956).
4. As described by E. E. Evans-Pritchard, *The Nuer* (1940), and P. P. Howell, *A Manual of Nuer Law* (1954).

larger and more complex governmental systems of, say, the Yoruba[5] or the Ashanti.[6] Fortes and Evans-Pritchard[7] put forward a triple classification of African societies into very small societies, larger kin-based acephalous societies, and centralized chiefly societies; but a crude division of this kind is (as the authors themselves would be the first to admit) no more than a temporary and provisional arrangement for purposes of description. In practice different African societies are located somewhere along the gamut or range of political organization, the polar elements of which might be represented by, say, the Bushmen at one end and the Ashanti or the Fulani-Hausa emirates of Northern Nigeria[8] at the other end. Even the major division into chiefless and chiefly societies, which has the attraction of simplicity, turns out in practice to oversimplify the reality; the first obstacle in the way of such a division being the inability to define "chief" in any meaningful way. (A typical example of a society—or rather, a group of societies —which does not fit exactly into either category is that of the Ibo of Eastern Nigeria; the controversy over whether they have or lack chiefs is still a live one.[9])

In these circumstances one might well ask, what are the possibilities of any unified statement of the institutions and practices of African societies in the domain of the present study; is not every generalization automatically invalidated? While one would admit, in reply to this objection, that there are manifest dangers in generalization, yet there is still a discoverable substratum of common features—common at least to a particular *type* of African society, though in some in-

5. See P. C. Lloyd, "The Traditional Political System of the Yoruba," 10 *S.W. Journal of Anthropology* (1954), 366; and P. C. Lloyd, *Yoruba Land Law* (1954).

6. Described by R. S. Rattray in his *Ashanti Law and Constitution* (1929) and elsewhere.

7. In their introduction to *African Political Systems.*

8. Cf. the description of the Hausa emirate of Zaria by M. G. Smith, in *Government in Zazzau, 1800-1950* (1960).

9. Cf. the report by G. I. Jones, *Report on the Position, Status and Influence of Chiefs and Natural Rulers of the Eastern Region of Nigeria* (1957).

stances common to all—which can be revealed by analysis; and it is with this substratum that we shall be presently concerned.[10] There are major divergences, though, especially in regard to the central question of the relationship between governor and governed, between (a) those societies where the governing authority is a kinsman of those who are governed (or the majority of them), where the number of the governed is so small that all can collect together for intimate discussions of public problems, and where the structures of government are rudimentary in the extreme, and (b) those societies where the kinship factor is no longer significant, where the explanation of the nexus between ruler and ruled is to be sought in a form of social contract, in conquest or in divine authority rather than in ties of blood, where the size of the society is much greater and the members of it can no longer conveniently collect together, and where the structures of government are complex and diversified or specialized.

II. *The Meaning of "The Rule of Law"*

It will doubtless appear somewhat bold to hope to define, in a short section of this paper, a term or concept whose meaning has been the subject of so much dispute among jurists for so long; indeed, the cynical and the skeptical would say that such dispute is vain and that the term is empty, meaningless and undefinable. Whether the present author agrees with any one of these schools of thought will perhaps emerge in a moment.

At the narrowest, the Rule of Law is taken to mean government by laws; it is thus placed in opposition, not only to government by men in the sense of government by the arbitrary will of a despotic individual or group, but to government by hazard, by the supernatural, even perhaps govern-

10. See also A. N. Allott, *Essays in African Law*, chap. iii, "The Unity of African Law," for a further discussion of the extent to which African customary laws are fundamentally uniform.

ment by immemorial custom. As law implies regularity and predictability, it is the contrary of government by whim or chance. In so far as it implies rational rules, it is the contrary of government by the irrational; in so far as it implies government by man-made rules, it is the contrary of government by divine or preternatural authorities or forces.

A second implication of the Rule of Law is commonly taken to be that no one is superior to the law, that the law applies to the ruler as well as (though not necessarily in exactly the same way as) to the ruled.

A third implication is that the law is impartially and equally administered, and that institutions exist for insuring this (e.g., a judiciary independent of the executive).

So much for the narrower, Diceyan, approach to the Rule of Law. Critics of it have pointed out, quite rightly, that on such a definition fascist dictatorships might be said to uphold the Rule of Law, since nothing is implied by this phrase as to the justice or morality of the content of the law. An enlarged definition of the Rule of Law, specifying an irreducible minimum of content, is thus put forward to meet this difficulty. The law must not only be equally applied; it must be just in itself and not infringe any of the prior fundamental rights of the citizens. Further attention is paid to the details of the *administration* of the law; the procedures of courts of justice, especially in criminal matters, must be fair and not prejudicial to any party, an accused must have the right to be represented by counsel, and so on. Not surprisingly this approach, with its emphasis on the procedural aspects of the Rule of Law, tends to find favor with the English common lawyer.[11]

11. A continuing discussion of both the theoretical and practical aspects of the Rule of Law in the modern world will be found in the publications of the International Commission of Jurists. Among those which are directly relevant to the present discussion are: *Report of the Proceedings of the African Conference on the Rule of Law, Lagos, Nigeria, January 3-7, 1961* (1961); the *Report of the Conclusions of the Delhi Congress*, in *Journal of I.C.J.* (1959), No. 1; and a discussion of the Lagos Conference in *Journal of the I.C.J.* (1961), No. 1.

But what are these prior fundamental rights, and how may they be discovered or formulated? A glance at such diverse documents as the United States Constitution, the Universal Declaration of Human Rights, or sections 18-33 of the Nigerian Constitution,[12] will supply lists of rights which different legislators have taken to be fundamental and to be abridged with difficulty or not at all. In general terms such lists extend to such matters as rights of free speech, freedom of movement, the right to hold property, and so on. As such, these statements are unobjectionable, provided it is realized that they are not so much formulations of legal rules as the outline of a political program. Statements of "fundamental rights" may be considered to go beyond their proper sphere once they descend to details, e.g., prescribing that everyone has the right to primary education up to a certain age.

How far it is possible to spell out similar principles in traditional African legal systems, and to what extent such principles have been expressly legislated into contemporary African constitutions, forms the major part of this inquiry.

III. *The Concept of Law in Traditional African Societies*

Before it is possible to discuss what the law is and how it functions in African societies, it is necessary to have some image in one's mind of the sort of thing one is looking for, but this clarification is not necessarily to be sought by attempting to answer the unanswerable, but frequently posed, question, "What is law?" It suffices if one has clearly in mind the kind of social manifestation in which one is interested, without committing oneself to any particular position in the unending verbal debate about law as such.

Examination of any society of men (and such examination need not be restricted to those which we might describe as

12. The Constitution of the Federation of Nigeria, Act No. 20 of 1963.

politically organized, and still less to anything which we label "state") shows that the members generally have expectations as to how each and any member will behave in particular situations. The word "expectations," as used here, cloaks an ambiguity: the members expect, both in the sense that they consider as probable and predictable and in the sense that they require, other members to behave in certain defined ways. Expectations as to behavior, in other words, are both predictive and normative.

Many of these expectations will be institutionalized and will be supported by social pressures to conform to them, and machinery or processes may exist for dealing with any deviation from them, or with any dispute to which such a deviation may give rise. But apart from the law as command or prohibition, we also have the law as facilitating or regulating the creation of social relationships, as giving efficacy to rearrangements of those relationships; and facultative rules or institutions also figure in the legal arrangements which we must investigate.[13]

It is therefore proposed to scrutinize African traditional societies with a view to discovering: (*i*) how far there are institutionalized expectations as to how a member of the society will or should behave in a given situation; (*ii*) how far such expectations are supported by social pressures to conform to them and to deal with any deviation from them; (*iii*) what institutionalized facilities there are for the creation of interpersonal relationships having specified consequences which are recognized and given social efficacy, with the corollary that certain other specified consequences will attach to the failure to make use of such facilities at appropriate opportunities; (*iv*) what sort of machinery there is for the formulation of rules specifying such expectations, facilities, and consequences (legislation; judicial decisions; custom); (*v*) whether

13. See the helpful analysis by H. L. A. Hart in *The Concept of Law* (1961), chap. iii.

there are approved processes for dealing with deviations from
such expectations, or for specifying in particular instances the
consequences of failure to use the appropriate facilities under
(*iii*) (self-help; arbitral and conciliation machinery; adjudication).

As space does not allow a full treatment of these points, it
can be briefly remarked that all African societies have institutionalized expectations about social behavior; that such expectations are supported by social pressures, though the
nature and effectiveness of the pressures vary; that every
African society has institutionalized facilities for such acts as
marriage or the distribution of a dead man's estate; but that
there is greater divergence once one comes to items (*iv*) and
(*v*) in our catalogue.

In the very small society (e.g., Bushmen), there appears to
be no overt machinery for the formulation of normative rules
of behavior; there is no legislature and no judiciary. In so far
as there are expectations about behavior, these derive from
custom, supernatural beliefs, or *ad hoc* agreement, promise,
or threat. In the larger acephalous society (e.g., the Kikuyu),
legislation exists but is of minor importance; while adjudication is found, specialization of function is at a relatively rudimentary stage: there are experts in adjudication rather than
judges. Most of the normative rules of behavior still derive
from custom and belief. In the chiefly society (e.g., the
Ashanti), there is usually formal machinery by which laws
can be made, though these must supplement, rather than replace, the bulk of the laws of customary origin. Equally there
is specialization of function in regard to adjudication, indeed,
the judge's function, apart from settling the case before him,
is often *jus dicere*, to state or restate the law for public instruction.[14]

There is equal variation with regard to the processes for

14. Cf. I. Schapera, "The Sources of Law in Tswana Tribal Courts: Legislation and Precedent," *Jour. of African Law*, I (1957), 150 ff., esp. at p. 161.

dealing with deviations or disputes; in the relatively unorganized society of the Nuer type,[15] the predominant modes of settling disputes are by self-help or by negotiation rather than by impartial adjudication. No central authority with power to enforce decisions may exist. But this assessment, though true of intergroup relations (where such groups are based on kinship, locality, or a mixture of the two), is rather misleading as far as intragroup relations are concerned. Where a deviation occurs affecting relations within, for instance, a lineage (where a society is organized on the lineage principle), then there may well be some person or body of persons having authority within such lineage and able to exert his authority to compel or persuade the recalcitrant to conform or make amends. (This question of authority and its consequences, both within and outside the kinship group, is discussed below in greater detail in the context of the relationship between the executive and the law.[16])

If one may generalize at this point, we find, as societies advance up the scale of complexity and size, that the machinery for the forcible correction of deviations from normative rules of behavior, or for imposing a solution of a dispute on the parties, becomes more effective and more readily employed. At the less advanced stage litigation is characteristically mediation, conciliation, arbitration, but at the more advanced stage adjudication. Courts in the more advanced societies can compel the attendance of parties and witnesses, punish crimes, and insure the execution of their sentences or orders. Despite this, we find many relics, even in the most advanced societies, of the arbitral approach to the settlement of disputes, and it remains a most important feature of the legal systems. This approach may express itself in two ways, either through the perpetuation of facilities for extrajudicial arbitration, or through the insinuation of an arbitral element

15. Cf. Howell, *op. cit.*, esp. at pp. 22 *et seq.*
16. In section IV below.

into the process of adjudication.[17] Because of the emphasis in some societies upon the necessity of persuading litigants to accept a judgment, and on the use of common sense and equity rather than strict legal rule to arrive at a decision, there have not been wanting those who have argued that law in any strict sense is entirely absent from such societies;[18] but this is, it is submitted, an exaggerated view, and even such societies have the features we have listed above under headings (*i*) to (*v*), which is all that we are concerned with now.

So much for the question of whether law, in any sense of the term, exists in African societies; but how is such law viewed? Is it considered the product of man's labors, or of something outside him? Is there any limit to what may be legislated in societies in which the possibility of conscious law-making exists?

In every African society the emphasis is on custom, morality, and religion as the sources of their laws; the rules of law exist because they have so existed from time immemorial and derive from the practice of the ancestors, or because they enshrine principles of universal morality prescribing how man ought to behave toward man, or because God has ordained them, or because they correspond to fundamental beliefs and taboos regarding the supernatural. In all chiefly societies, and in some of those without chiefs, a legislative power exists, but such power ought to be exercised within the limits of what is right and reasonable and fits in with the religious and moral system of the people. A powerful sanction insuring that legislation would conform in this way was present in most societies, inasmuch as a chief or ruling clique could not promulgate a new edict without the concurrence of the people or their representatives, who would surely object if their fundamental beliefs and expectations were in-

17. Cf. M. Gluckman, *The Judicial Process among the Barotse of Northern Rhodesia* (1955), *passim*.
18. E.g., M. J. Field in *Akim-Kotoku* (1948).

fringed. (This is further discussed and illustrated below, where the legislature and the law are examined.)

Much of the law-making in an African society is not by legislation in the formal sense, but rather through the process of dispute-settling and as a by-product of it. Every successful arbitration or conciliation tends to set a standard by which future relations will be regulated, while the judge in his adjudication has the scope and the power to develop new laws for new needs or to meet new problems. In both kinds of process the voice of the people may be heard; thus in many African societies the people generally have the right to attend, and if necessary participate in, a public adjudication. If a judge should put forward a rule which did not meet with public favor, the public would thus have an opportunity to say so.

IV. *The Executive and the Law*

What is the nature of the relation between the supreme administering authority and the law? To what extent do the people have a say in the processes of government and in the administration of the law? How far is there differentiation of functions and separation of powers in African society?

It may be convenient to start with the last question. It is generally accepted that neither the practice nor the doctrine of separation of powers finds any place in traditional African societies. Commonly an administering authority will tend to be the supreme executive, judge, law-giver, war-leader, and perhaps priest. All decisions will be made in his name, and he will be the final court of appeal in judicial as well as in administrative matters. This is as true of the head of the family group or local headman as it is of a paramount chief. The notion that a ruler should voluntarily abstain from ruling in some sphere would strike the traditional authorities as absurd. So much for the theory; but in practice, especially in the more complex societies, a good deal of specialization existed. For example, there might be a class of "professional" judges or legal experts; despite the fact that they would give their judgments in the name of the ruler whom they represented, customary law might deprecate too direct an intervention in proceedings by the ruler himself. Thus Rattray reports for old Ashanti that:

> In court, his [the Chief's] role was and is that of a judge who sits and permits others to do most of the talking, he himself only interfering at times to correct some irregularity or to guide the case. An *Ohene okyeame,* i.e., a Chief who takes upon himself the duties of his *Okyeame* (Spokesman and prosecutor), was and is a term of opprobrium all over Ashanti.[19]

Despite the theoretical concentration of power in the hands of a single ruler in the chiefly societies, in practice the tribal constitution was usually an intricate structure incorporating highly effective checks and balances on his power. These checks and balances consisted in (*i*) the limiting effect of the tribal constitution and legal system, to which the ruler was subject as much as anyone (even if in a personally privileged position), (*ii*) the decentralization and distribution of power among many subordinate authorities, and (*iii*) the inherent power of the people to control the actions of their ruler.

The first point cannot be better illustrated than by a further citation from Rattray, who says:

> In spite of the reverence and religious awe in which his [the Chief's] person was held, his subjects had nevertheless very distinct ideas as to the manner in which he should exercise his authority. . . . A Chief's duties and limitations are strictly defined by a whole series of instructions (which are publicly recited before him on the occasion of his enstoolment).
>
> . . . To all outward appearance and to superficial observers, who included the populace, the Chief was an autocrat. In reality every move and command which appeared to emanate from his mouth had been discussed in private and been previously agreed upon by his councillors, to whom everyone in the tribe had

19. *Ashanti Law and Constitution,* p. 81.

access and to whom popular opinion of any subject was thus known. Such, at any rate, was the ideal; serious departure from this custom would eventually lead to destoolment. Although nominally the Ashanti Constitution was intended to appear to be autocratic, in correct practice it was democratic to a degree.[20]

Again, in connection with our second point, a paramount chief might appear to be in an autocratic position as the supreme fount of authority; in practice, in states organized upon the hierarchical system, much of his authority was delegated to, or limited by that of, his subordinates.

And lastly, the people in most places retained a right of control over their rulers. In some societies (such as that of the Ashanti), this right was a direct one, sanctioned by the power of the people to depose a ruler who behaved unconstitutionally or ill-advisedly. Elsewhere popular pressure might be exerted through the councilors of the ruler; if the ruler misused his position, he might be deposed by them or, as in the Yoruba system, the chiefs who were the *oba*'s (king's) councilors could "ask him to die."[21] Where the constitution did not even provide a remedy of this sort, the people might "vote with their feet" by seceding or by rebelling.[22]

We may express the point which has just been made thus: if we look for separation of powers in the modern European sense, we shall find none of it in traditional African societies; but if we are willing to accept that there are other ways by which power may be fragmented, distributed and balanced, then this is typical of African society. The separation of powers is horizontal, i.e., by rank, rather than vertical, i.e., by function.

It is the same with the question of the participation of the people in the process of government. The notion of a "legislature" as a distinct constitutional entity, whose members are chosen by and are representative of the voters, and which is

20. *Ibid.*, 81-83; see also pp. 405-408.
21. Cf. Lloyd, *Yoruba Land Law*, p. 46.
22. Cf. H. Ashton, *The Basuto* (1952), p. 217.

answerable to the electorate, does not usually exist in African societies. The discussions, for instance, on delegated legislation, which occupy such an important place in the proceedings of the Delhi congress of the International Commission of Jurists,[23] are utterly irrelevant to traditional African governments. Nor need importance be attached to "elected" government, provided government is "responsible" in the sense that it is subject to the assent and control of the people governed.

In some societies (e.g., the Basuto[24] or the Tswana[25]) there was direct participation by every adult male in the process of law-making through annual assemblies of the people, where all could participate and accept, or in theory reject, projects of laws submitted by the ruler. Elsewhere such direct democracy is absent, except in some of the smaller kin-based societies.[26] In its place there is a reliance on the notions of conciliar and representative government. Every ruler is advised by a council, and cannot act on his own initiative; the members of the council are usually representative of different sections of the community, though they hold their office by descent and not necessarily by popular election. Decisions can be communicated downwards through the chain of representation; complaints and proposals can similarly be communicated upwards. The result, especially where popular control is reinforced by a power to depose an unpopular ruler or councilor, is effectively "democratic."

One may put it this way: the right to rule is often seen as flowing from and expressing the will of the people. The person or group which exercises this right may be designated by the people in some societies, or may occupy this position by divine right, inheritance, or appointment from above in other societies. But close analysis generally shows that it is only the

23. *Supra*, n. 11.
24. Cf. Ashton, *op. cit.*, pp. 215 *et seq.*
25. I. Schapera, *Handbook of Tswana Law and Custom* (2nd ed., 1955), at pp. 80 *et seq.*
26. E.g., the Kikuyu.

title to authority which derives from position; the *authority itself* derives from an express or implied mandate or "social contract" with the subjects. A family or lineage head in West Africa may be chosen by the family and thereafter exercise authority within the family, but it is the family's authority that is exercised.[27]

V. *The Legislative Power and the Law*

Sufficient has already been said to indicate that there is little use in looking for distinct legislatures in African society. This does not mean that there are not legislative councils or meetings, or, failing these, legislative procedures. In many of the chiefly societies, the chief had the power to promulgate new edicts in and through his council, and such matters would usually be thoroughly discussed first by the councilors before they would go forth as the command of the chief. The decisions of such councils or meetings were often subject to popular approval in one form or another, at least in a negative sense. But even though legislation was to a certain extent controlled by the people, it would be wrong to think that all the people, equally and without discrimination on the basis of sex, race, age, social position, etc., participated in the process of government and law-making. Nothing could be farther from the truth. The principle of "one man one vote" is in this sense entirely foreign to Africa; and the typical African arrangement would be a differential or qualitative franchise, for African society is characterized by the existence of differential statuses—of rank (as between chief, councilor, freeman, slave); of sex (as between males and females); of seniority (as between elders, family heads, married men, minors); of ethnic origin (as between native-born citizens, strangers, servile substrata); even, in some areas, of wealth. A man's opinion was esteemed more

27. Cf. Lloyd, *Yoruba Land Law*, p. 83.

highly, and he would be permitted to express it more freely, if he came from one of the upper categories rather than from one of the lower. Women were almost entirely excluded from the governmental system. In many areas it was the family or household heads, rather than the individuals as such, who constituted the free "electorate."

On the other hand, many African societies adhere to the principle of "to every man a voice." It is characteristic that persons, especially those who might be prejudicially affected by a possible act or decision, should have the opportunity of speaking out on the matter. The emphasis on conciliatory and arbitral modes of settling disputes is a good illustration of this attitude; let the parties each put his case, and let the talk go on till everyone feels that every conceivable argument has been put, till a consensus of opinion can emerge.

The same principle is also enshrined in the common African emphasis on the necessity of unanimity in decision-making. The whole concept of majority decision, so much esteemed by the West as the embodiment of the democratic principle, would appear grossly tyrannical in many traditional African societies, even at the present day. If there is opposition, then the remedy is not to outvote it, but to persuade it.

It may be helpful if one or two instances of the legislative process in action are given here:

Among the Kikuyu and Meru as described by Lambert:[28]

Legislation is a function of the senior lodge or the senior rank of the elders' lodge. [The *Kikuyu* are acephalous, and rule is by "elders" of a certain grade or generation.] . . . Theoretically the members of the senior lodge or rank who are also members of the ruling age or generation are the legislative body as long as their age or generation is in power. But in practice the lodge does not allow this splitting of itself into two functionally distinct divisions. *Athamaki* or *agambi* [prominent or leading councilors] of the ruling generation (real or artificial) may proclaim the law but they will rarely have been solely responsible for the passing of it. . . . A law passed and promulgated by the ruling grade alone would have the force of law during its rule, but not

28. *Op. cit.,* p. 131.

a moment longer. There would probably be a deliberate repeal of it in fact when the following grade assumed the right to govern at the next *ntuiko* [handing over of power to the next generation].

Laws and specific orders are usually proclaimed at public meetings by *athamaki* or *agambi* of the ruling generation or set supported by those of the other alternation. [Especially is there revision and restatement of the laws at the coming in of a new generation]. . . . The sanctions in support of these laws are largely of a supernatural nature.[29]

Legislation in Meru[30] is by the appropriate *njuri* or elders' council of the area. The whole tribe might be represented by a *nkireba* or select committee of elders representative of all the constituent areas. There are, both in Kikuyu and Meru, limits on the legislative power: thus some areas hold that purely domestic matters, e.g., regulation of "bride-price," are outside the competence of the legislative authorities.[31]

And for the Basuto (who have a strong centralized chieftaincy), Ashton reports that in the old days:

The chief may decide all minor matters on his own responsibility, with or against the advice of his councillors, but all matters of importance should first be discussed with the people at a public meeting (*pitso*), to which all adult males are summoned. . . . *Pitsos* were frequently called by Moshesh and other chiefs [in the nineteenth century]. . . . Discussion, according to contemporary observers, was keen, great freedom of speech was allowed, and great weight attached to the opinion and attitude of the people.[32]

The chief could not afford to disregard the advice or wishes of the people: *morena ke morena ka batho* ("the chief is the chief by the people").

On the other side of Africa, in the old kingdom of Ashanti as reported by Rattray, the position was similar:

To all outward appearances and to the superficial observer, the fiction indeed was often encouraged that he [the chief] was a despot and an autocrat. In reality, every move, every command

29. *Ibid.*, pp. 136-138.
30. *Ibid.*, pp. 139-140.
31. *Ibid.*, pp. 140 *et seq.*
32. *Op. cit.*, pp. 215-217.

which appeared to emanate from his mouth, had been discussed and agreed upon in private by every councillor who had a say in the affairs of State. These councillors, in turn, would also have taken care to sound *their* subjects right down to the *Asafo*. Nominally autocratic, the Akan constitution was in practice democratic to a degree. . . .

We pride ourselves, I believe, on being a democratic people and flatter ourselves that our institutions are of a like nature. An Ashanti who was familiar with his own and our Constitution would deny absolutely our right to apply this term either to ourselves or to our Constitution. To him a democracy implies that the affairs of the Tribe (State) must rest, not in the keeping of the few, but in the hands of the many. . . . To him the State is literally a *Res Publica;* it is everyone's business.[33]

VI. *Adjudication and the Law*

Several distinct types of process are found in African societies by which disputes may be settled, deviations from the norm remedied, or justice obtained. Some of these processes are extrajudicial, e.g., self-help; but this does not mean that they are extralegal, as commonly the permissible limits of such remedial action are set by law. Apart from these, we may find, in the tribes lacking a central authority, that most disputes are settled by negotiation before competent arbitrators, though there may also be some offenses so shocking that the community itself reacts in order to suppress them; among procedures for dealing with these is the Kikuyu *king'ole*.[34] It would be quite erroneous to call this sort of procedure "lynch law,"[35] since it is not lawless and in despite of the law, but in fulfilment of it, and carries with it the social approval both of the people at large and of those in charge of its government.

The emphasis on arbitration and judgments by consent has already been referred to. Such emphasis becomes of less im-

33. *Op. cit.,* p. 406.
34. Lambert, *op. cit.,* p. 79.
35. As it is described by G. Lindblom in his *The Akamba* (1920), at pp. 176 *et seq.*

portance once there is a strong political authority able to enforce its decisions. In such societies the judicial process becomes of relatively more importance than the arbitral, though
many cases which come before a court may have been the
previous subject of negotiations outside the court, and a court
may use its influence to promote a reconciliation between the
parties.

The importance attached today to the procedural aspects
of the Rule of Law means that there are many possible con-
traventions of the Rule of Law that might occur in this field.
Indeed, once traditional African societies were incorporated
in the colonial system, pressure was exerted at this point (by
review of the functioning of the indigenous tribunals) to insure a more just content and application of the customary
law.

The first point which may be picked out for special examination is that mentioned in the report of the conclusions of
the Delhi conference on the Rule of Law:

> It is always important that the definition and interpretation of
> the law should be as certain as possible, and this is of particular
> importance in the case of the criminal law, where the citizen's
> life or liberty may be at stake. Certainty cannot exist in the
> criminal law where the law, or the penalty for its breach, is
> retrospective.[36]

How far was or is African customary law, especially the criminal law, certain in its definition or interpretation?

In some societies offenses and their penalties are stated with
great particularity; e.g., so many goats for one sort of wound-
ing, another figure for a different sort.[37] In other societies,
especially those which had fallen under a tyranny (as with
nineteenth-century Buganda[38] or the Zulu[39] under Chaka),

36. *Supra,* n. 11.
37. Cf. Lambert, *op. cit.,* p. 119; Howell, *op. cit.,* pp. 669-670; Lindblom,
op. cit., p. 156.
38. Described in E. S. Haydon, *Law and Justice in Buganda* (1960), at
pp. 4-5.
39. For an account of the Zulu system, see M. Gluckman, "The Kingdom
of the Zulu of South Africa," in *African Political Systems, op. cit.*

the criminal law was completely unpredictable and represented little more than the whim of the ruler.

It is a fair comment to say that in general the rules of customary law were less precisely formulated than they are in modern Western systems. But to admit this is by no means to admit that there were no rules at all.

There is another aspect of criminal trials brought out in the Delhi Conclusions: "The application of the Rule of Law involves an acceptance of the principle that an accused person is assumed to be innocent until he has been proved to be guilty."[40] How far does African customary law recognize any presumption of innocence? This is a difficult question to answer. Speaking generally, one might say that the principle is qualified in African practice by the common assumption that if an incriminating circumstance appears to attach to a particular individual, this creates a presumption which it will be up to him to displace. Sometimes such an incriminating circumstance is one which would be recognized as such by Europeans as well: if a man is seen leaving a married woman's quarters in a furtive manner, this may give rise to a presumption that he has been misconducting himself with her. But at other times the so-called incriminating circumstance, or the method of determining that it is incriminating, is unintelligible and unacceptable to the Western mind. Thus certain harmful occurrences may be laid at the door of someone who is believed to have procured them by malevolent witchcraft: it may be up to him to disprove that he is responsible. Or resort may be had to divination in order to determine who is responsible for harm; such a procedure cannot be called a fair trial in any sense of the term, even though the supernatural forces to which appeal is made may well be neutral as between the contestants or different suspects. But one could argue that the fundamental principle or presumption of innocence remains; all that is different are the theories

40. *Supra*, n. 11.

of causation of harm, or the methods of determining guilt. (And is there such a profound difference, if one views the matter in the context of the belief-systems of the two peoples concerned, between the appeal to a diviner in an African society, and the calling in of, say, a court medical expert in the English system?)

It is interesting to note that the Delhi Conclusions went on to qualify the presumption of innocence: "An acceptance of this general principle is not inconsistent with provisions of law which, in particular cases, shift the burden of proof once certain facts creating a contrary presumption have been established."[41] The remarks made above about the African attitude to such a presumption could well be brought within the terms of this proviso.

The formula, "a man is presumed innocent until he is proved guilty," does not always exactly fit the spirit and procedures of African customary law for another reason: this reason lies in the use of the term "guilty." African legal procedure may be concerned with establishing *responsibility* for a wrong—who is answerable for this harm?—rather than in measuring the *guilt* of an accused. Causation and not blameworthiness is often the important point. Did this man cause this harm? If so, then he is answerable for it. Thus Gluckman comments for the Lozi:

> The Lozi hold that it is self-evident that a man must be convicted by strong evidence, or that civil disputes are decided by the weight of the evidence. . . . Their standard of negligence is indeed so high that it appears as if their law does not recognize moral guilt in assessing damage, as has been frequently stated for all primitive law. Responsibility appears to be absolute.[42]

(However Gluckman goes on to show that the Lozi do show regard for culpability in certain cases.) But the position is utterly different in a society like the Nuer, an acephalous society with no central authority capable of adjudicating on

41. *Supra*, n. 11.
42. *Op. cit.*, p. 205.

the merits of a dispute; here—in the traditional system—the fact that a member of one group has inflicted harm on a member of another group is more important than the question whether he intended to inflict the harm, or was negligent in doing so.[43]

A further assertion about the content of the Rule of Law in connection with criminal trials will cause more difficulty if it is applied to African legal systems:

> The Rule of Law requires that an accused person should have adequate opportunity to prepare his defence and this involves:
> (1) That he should at all times be entitled to the assistance of a legal adviser of his own choice. . . .[44]

In practically no African society was there a distinct corps of professional legal advisers or advocates. The notion of legal representation *in this sense* is foreign to African law. But in another sense the notion of legal representation in judicial proceedings is central to African law. In very many societies, an individual against whom legal complaint is made has the right to call in someone close to him—perhaps the head of his family or other senior relative—to speak on his behalf or to advise him as to the conduct of his case. In some areas a "family" or other kinship group would contain one or two members who had distinguished themselves as advocates in this way, and who would come to the assistance of a fellow-member involved in legal proceedings. And in many societies a wrong committed by an individual created liability in the group of which he was a member; not merely was the wrongdoer in such a case represented by the authorities of his kinship group, but his place as principal was taken by the group itself. In other words, an accused man (if he was a native of the place and not a foreigner) would not usually go friendless into court. A similar result to that desired by the modern proponents of the Rule of Law was achieved by other means.

43. Cf. Howell, *op. cit.*, pp. 41-42.
44. *Supra*, n. 11.

What about the trial itself? We commonly accept the idea that there are certain rules which must be followed to insure that there is a fair trial. Some of these rules are subsumed in the requirements of "natural justice" as defined by the English courts; no man is to be condemned without being told the offense of which he is accused, or without being heard in his own defense; no man is to be a judge in his own cause; there must be equality of treatment before the law; and so on. Are such requirements found in African customary legal systems?

The answer is that they are found, but imperfectly. Thus, in general, a man is not condemned unheard, but the sort of procedure found in the Kikuyu *king'ole*,[45] where an accused would know nothing of the proceedings against him until he was lured into the forest and put to death, infringes this principle. And occasions arose where a man would be judge in his own cause: e.g., where a chief was personally involved in a case, as in trying a breach of his own order or an accusation of adultery with one of his own wives.

Where a ruler, whether superior or subordinate, himself does wrong, he may in most societies be tried or proceeded against in some way or another. In some places a ruler may be tried in his own court (e.g., with a ward headman among the Tswana[46]); elsewhere this may be reckoned a contradiction—as with the Lozi, of whom Gluckman says:

> Rulers should be bound by the law, and under Lozi law can do wrong and be tried by courts. But the heads of courts should not be tried by their own courts, for no man should be a judge in his own cause and therefore the "owner" of the court cannot be tried in it.[47]

There are, however, political or constitutional sanctions against a ruler whose behavior offends and who is not amenable to legal proceeding.

As for equality before the law, some types of inequality have

45. Lambert, *op. cit.*, p. 79.
46. Cf. Schapera, p. 282.
47. *Op. cit.*, p. 27.

already been referred to (e.g., the inferior status of women, minors, foreigners, commoners). But in another sense it could be argued that, in all those customary laws where litigation became a matter between the respective families or kinship groups of complainant and wrongdoer, equality between the parties to a court case was insured, since the contest would be between families of equal rank, and not between individuals of varying rank.

VII. *Fundamental and Inalienable Rights*

To what extent did the notion that citizens enjoy certain rights which cannot be overridden by positive legislation or by executive action exist in African societies? The typical Western list, one echoed in modern constitutional documents, includes such freedoms as freedom of religious belief, freedom of speech, freedom of assembly, and freedom of movement. Is there a similar list in African societies?

The constitutions and legal systems of most traditional African societies appear to be based on three principles: *mos,* the custom of the people; *jus,* the idea of justice or right morality; and *fas,* the divinely ordained or supernatural law. *Lex,* humanly made law, is in general only allowable in so far as it does not fundamentally contradict or set aside *mos, jus* and *fas;* the ambit of the legislative power is restricted.

Quite apart from this, there is a continuous restriction upon the power of the ruler or law-giver which prevents his trespassing on the fundamental rights of his subjects; this is imposed by the fact that government, as we have seen above, rests partly on inherent right to rule and partly on the consent of the governed. The subjects often have the means to reject or reverse laws, orders, decisions, or actions of which they fundamentally disapprove.

In no society outside Africa will an unqualified right to freedom of speech or of association be found; the same is true of African societies. Rules forbidding seditious activity, disturbance of the peace, insult, blasphemy, will be found in African just as in English society. The picture that we sometimes derive from outside observers, however, of a custom- and chief-ridden peasantry, automatically carrying out without protest whatever superstition or a dictatorial chief requires, is often remote from the truth.

This does not mean—one must hasten to add—that existence, thought, and action in African society were free and untrammelled. Severe limits were placed on allowable activity. For example, protests about iniquitous rule were usually intended to change the ruler, and not the system of government. There was little or no sense of freedom of thought or religion: a tribesman had to accept the tribal religion as he found it. Nevertheless, revolutions were possible and are recorded; great innovators, such as Okomfo Anokye in Ashanti,[48] could devise a new state religion; Islam spread widely and was tolerated; economic and social progress was made through the work of those bold spirits who planted new crops or adopted new customs.

The right to form associations did not go as far as modern Western theories might wish; the concept of an opposition, in the sense of an organized group or party legitimately endeavoring to substitute itself for the existing governing group, was completely unknown. One could accurately say that African traditional societies were one-party, or perhaps no-party, states. But this gives by no means all of the picture. Situations where there was organized or institutionalized opposition are frequent. In some societies the opposition is due to tension between groups or areas of different ethnic origin; in other societies one has what one may call factionalism in ruling circles, with different lineages or factions competing for power. In some African constitutions, the paramount chief finds himself confronted by an official who acts

48. For whom see Rattray, *op. cit.*, at pp. 270 *et seq.*

as the recognized spokesman of the people, his (the chief's) subjects.[49]

VIII. *The Rule of Law in Modern African Societies*

I turn now to consider some of the implications of the features of traditional societies, which we have just outlined, for the construction and functioning of modern African constitutions. Both in the French-speaking and in the English-speaking sectors the colonial powers (France, Belgium, and Britain) endowed their newly independent ex-colonies with political and legal institutions which were close copies of those prevailing in the mother-countries at the time, and hence "democratic" in a narrow European sense. Sometimes the colonial power went further, and purported to write into and entrench in the African constitutions provisions which restated and protected the fundamental rights and liberties implied by the Rule of Law (as with Nigeria and Sierra Leone).

The present position in Africa, it is well known, does not reflect these facts. In most states opposition, in the sense of a politically organized party, or the possibility of one, has voluntarily evaporated or been compulsorily eliminated. Thus countries like Ghana and Tanganyika have formally declared their adherence to the notion of the one-party state. Legislation or executive action appearing to infringe freedom of speech, liberty of movement, or freedom from arbitrary arrest, is all too frequent. There are suspicions that the judiciary, which in many of the new African states was carefully insulated from political influence, may now or in the near future fall under political control. Is there any hope for the Rule of Law in such circumstances?

Justification offered for these moves usually rests on two

49. E.g., the *mankrado* or *osomanyawa* in Ghanaian societies; cf. J. B. Danquah, *Akan Laws and Customs* (1928), pp. 37-38.

assertions: that a newly emerging and rapidly developing country cannot afford the dissipation and distraction of its energies which a fully democratic system, complete with two-party legislature, necessarily involves, and that in any case these imported notions are "un-African," and that the new political and legal structures which are being created more closely reflect traditional African institutions and attitudes./ I shall not argue the first point now, which is a theme for political scientists rather than lawyers, but it is worthwhile taking a closer look at the second.

One of the more thoroughgoing of the Africanizing governments is that of Ghana; and their present system of presidential government bears many resemblances to the traditional Akan system of government by the paramount chief in council (which we have already discussed as it is manifested in Ashanti). But there are also many dissimilarities. Despite the republican constitution, it is doubtful whether the citizens of Ghana can change or depose their rulers, either at the higher or the lower levels, as easily as under the traditional system, nor are Rattray's remarks about the chief (quoted above) descriptive of the present system of cabinet government in Ghana. The power to appoint judges is firmly in the hands of the president. The same was true of the Akan constitution to a limited extent: chiefs, councilors, village headmen, and others with judicial functions owed their position more to the fact that they had been elected by their people or the representatives of their people than to nomination by their overlord. If one tried to adopt an equivalent of this arrangement in a modern African state, one would probably come up with a system of election of judges as in the United States.

Our examination of the extent to which the ideas of the Rule of Law were incorporated and observed in the traditional African modes of government underlines one vital point, that it is essential to look at the substance rather than the form of the institutions in order to evaluate their tendencies and merits, and we saw that African institutions generally looked better the more closely they were examined. The same, it is comforting to remember, may also be true of contemporary Africa. The Rule of Law, in any real sense of the phrase, is a part of indigenous African law; it would be reassuring if the governments of Africa, especially those which wish to build on their own precious cultural heritage, were able to translate the rules and practices of their own customary laws into modern terms.

THE FORTUNES OF CONSTITUTIONAL GOVERNMENT IN THE POLITICAL DEVELOPMENT OF THE NEW STATES

Edward Shils

There are no new states in Asia or Africa, whether monarchies or republics, in which the elites who demanded independence did not, at the moment just prior to their success, believe that self-government and democratic government were identical. For the most part, they believed that democratic self-government entailed the full paraphernalia of the modern polity, viz.: popular sovereignty expressed through elections in which various parties would contend with one another for the support of a universal electorate, a legislative body under the dominance of the majority party, the freedom of the individual to express himself, a free press, the rule of law, the right of association, and the subordination of the military to the civil arm. British ideas of liberty and the principles of 1789 were in their minds. Unlike the European nationalists of the nineteenth century who were also mainly liberals and constitutionalists and unlike those who had the upper hand in the early years of the nationalist movements in Asia and Africa, the elites of the newly sovereign Asian and African states have on the whole not been liberals in the old sense. They have been largely socialistic in outlook but they did not believe that there was any incompatibility between their liberal-democratic political views and their socialistic views about economic organization and policy. For the most part, their minds were quite vague about the exact contours of the self-governing regimes which they wished to establish. Their minds were formed largely by the democratic socialist outlook which was common in Europe in the first third of the present century and which did not find it impossible to maintain some sympathy with Soviet communism.

I

Ever since the American Revolution, the act of creating a state has tended to entail the declaration of the fundamental law of the new country in the form of a constitution. The process of constitution-making has been regarded as a major symbol of the formation of the new state. It has probably been no less significant to the constitution-makers of the post-colonial new states of Asia and Africa than it was to the lawyers and politicians of the West when they attempted to crystallize their liberties. Having become independent, a population living in a bounded territory becomes a state by the promulgation of a constitution. In the new states, the making of a constitution is even more important because it asserts the existence of the society by the formation of the state. Constitutionalism, because of its tradition, almost automatically entails some limitations of the powers of governments and some assurance of the rights of the citizenry which it creates.

The constitutions of the new states—and in many instances the proto-constitutions, i.e., the constituting instruments of establishment whereby their formal imperial rulers acknowledged the sovereignty of the once colonial territory—have quite normally envisaged democratic, and therefore representative, equalitarian, law-bound regimes with ample provision for individual and public liberties. There is no new state in Asia or Africa which does not have or which did not begin with the intention of having a written constitution which defined the powers of the government, which regulated the powers of the executive, and which guaranteed the liberties of the subject.

The constitutions of the new states were of a "Western type." They drew much from British practice and from the written constitutions of the United States, Ireland, Holland, France, and Australia. They were such because the politicians of the nationalist movement wished to be like those states from which they were trying to free themselves, because they vaguely assumed that the sovereign states which they were hoping to establish would be democratic regimes, and also because those experts who were given the task of drafting the constitutions were trained in Western-type law and legal draftsmanship. It was their inspiration which was precipitated in the constitutions of the Asian states.

There is a further reason for this. The new states intended to escape from the autocracy of colonial government. In wishing to guarantee the control of the sovereign electorate, they had to specify and confine the powers of government. They guaranteed the right to free political choice and the free expression of opinion on political matters. Practically every new state in Asia and Africa has begun its career with the acceptance of a multi- or bi-party system, with provisions for the freedom of association and for the liberty of the individual to express himself in political matters.

In many cases the constitution has remained unaltered in written form and has not been formally amended or replaced. Yet most of the new states have, in practice, seriously deviated from this original, actual, or intended constitution. The deviations which have taken place in practice have, in the main, been legitimated by reference to certain exceptional clauses in the constitution or else in disregard of the constitution. There are only a few instances of an explicit abrogation of the constitution and its replacement by another fundamental law (Pakistan, Indonesia). But whatever the mode of legitimation, dissenting political parties have been suppressed or forced to amalgamate with ruling parties; newspapers have been placed under censorship or otherwise controlled or suppressed; editors and journalists, politicians, and private citizens have been imprisoned, confined by domiciliary detention or deported; ethnic, religious, and linguistic minorities have been persecuted.

One of the major functions of a constitution is to solve in an orderly and peaceful manner the problem of succession for societies which do not believe in an inherited right to rule. The constitutional principle of succession has been frequently infringed in the new states. In at least seven of the new states (Pakistan, Ceylon, Togoland, Iraq, Syria, Burma, South Viet-Nam) assassination has been resorted to as a means of removing leading politicians from office; in others, there have been attempts at assassination or trials for conspiracies to assassinate (Indonesia, Ivory Coast, Ceylon, Ghana, Jordan, Tunisia).[1]

In about a dozen states (Indonesia, Burma, Pakistan, Sudan, Iraq, Syria, Egypt, South Korea, Laos, Togoland, Algeria), there have been unconstitutional interventions of the military into politics, peremptory subversions by the military of the constitutionally established mode of succession, and the establishment of the superiority of the constitutionally subordinated, executive branch over the rest of the governmental

1. The new succession problem is one of the most serious for the new states. It is one which the availability of pre-eminent charismatic personalities has allowed states like India, Egypt, Ghana, and Indonesia to evade by the simple device of continuance in office of the great figure of the "revolution." (India did this fully within the limits of the constitutional system. The others are less constitutional.) In Ceylon, the assassinated Prime Minister was succeeded by his wife, following a legitimate procedure. In Burma, there had been, except for a brief interlude, only one Prime Minister until the Army displaced him in an unconstitutional manner. Throughout the Middle East, the succession where it has occurred has not been through an orderly constitutional process, not even in Lebanon where a mild civil war preceded the resignation of one president and the constitutional accession of his successor.

system. Several states (Congo, Indonesia, Iraq) have had civil wars. Others, even without civil war, have experienced "states of emergency" (Ceylon, Nigeria).

Yet none of the new states of Asia or Africa is totalitarian except for North Viet-Nam and Northern Korea. None is even thoroughly oligarchical except for Guinea, Egypt, and Ghana. The oligarchical regimes which have been established are frequently fragmentary and incomplete. Just as the constitutional system of the new states retained elements, liberal as well as illiberal, of the colonial regimes which preceded them, so the quasi-oligarchical regimes have permitted a modest amount of liberty to survive. In Ceylon, during the Emergency of 1958, there were persons who criticized the government's conduct and the emergency was rescinded after a time. In Indonesia's guided democracy, certain political parties are allowed to continue their limited existence. In Algeria, when the President of the Assembly recently resigned in protest against the new constitution which is a charter for an unconfined one-party oligarchy, he accompanied his resignation with a public criticism of the constitution. In Ghana, despite the application of the Preventative Detention Act to many members of the opposition, several trials for conspiracy to overthrow the government, and an egregious intervention by the president into university personnel and academic policy, the university still retains a considerable measure of academic freedom. In Pakistan, during the period of martial law, the government did not suppress all criticism; it has arrested very few of its political opponents and has left the universities alone, but not the press. Of course, to some extent, these fragments of liberty are the legacy of the administrative incompetence of the oligarchy, of its incapacity to extend its control as far as it wishes. In other instances, they testify to the *ad hoc*, undoctrinaire nature of the oligarchy. In some cases, they testify to the inhibitions which a fragmentary liberalism still activates in the elites who began as democrats and have arrived at oligarchy.

II

The conception of the modern order, with which elites of the new states began, envisaged a regime of justice—an egalitarian, substantive justice as well as formal equality before the law. It expressed a concern for the will and well-being of "the people"—popular sovereignty and a higher standard of living through improved technology. It required rationality —a rational administration and public policy based upon factual knowledge and disciplined judgment. It looked to the formation of a nation with a distinctive identity—created by the nurture of indigenous cultural traditions and the practice of modern culture, scientific and literary, as well as through a wide sharing in these cultural attainments by the whole people. The elites of the new states wanted this modern order, intimately associated with the idea of the nation, to be esteemed by other countries throughout the world and they were convinced that this esteem could not be merited or obtained if they did not modernize themselves. Monarchies as well as republics shared these views.

The existence of the United Nations has intensified these preoccupations because it has given the new states opportunities for continuous representation in the most public forum before the judgment of the more advanced powers.[2]

These diverse, primarily modern, goals are not necessarily fully compatible with each other. Conflicts of interest among

2. For the most part, they did not give much thought to their traditional cultural inheritance; their traditional social practices did not figure prominently in their conception of their own future. Attention was given to the vernacular languages but religion was not accorded equal prominence. Only Pakistan began with a religious legitimation but there, too, the constitution of 1956, although acknowledging the Islamic foundation of the state, was a modern, liberal democratic, secular document. The other Islamic states, although referring frequently to the glories of Islam and the need for its renascence, did not strive for an Islamic future.

different groups who attach more weight to some than to others, differences in the strength of attachments to one rather than to another of the ends, have meant that in the intense situation of real political life, some would be renounced and others would be emphasized in speech more than in deed. Some would be jettisoned in silence; others would come forward to priority. The strain of the attempt to exercise authority through the flimsy machinery of an embryonically modern state has raised questions in the minds of members of the elites about how essential some of their original goals were in the total set of the goals with which they began their political careers. The more shallowly rooted tended to be discarded more easily or at least put aside for future consideration. Certain latent goals, which had not been accorded any important programmatic significance began to emerge once the new state passed from the condition of a program to political reality.

III

The raw materials with which the elites of the new states have had to conduct their affairs have not been propitious to the realization of the programs to which they were committed by their constitutions and their ambitions. The institutions, the technology, the cultural beliefs of the mass of their fellow-citizens have not been to their taste. The attainment of the goals of a modern society, a modern culture, and a modern polity would require a deep and broad transformation of the inheritance which the past of their fellow citizens has imposed upon them. In general, in degrees which varied from country to country and within each country, they wanted to escape from that past, or at least free themselves from what they thought were its extrinsic features. They have not been able to do so.

Other, less indigenous parts of their inheritance from the colonial age kept them from becoming as modern and as liberal as they wished to become originally. Large foreign-owned commercial firms; peasant and plantation agriculture; the predominance of the production of a few raw materials for a world market; dependence on European centers of manufacturing for manufactured products; low per capita incomes; numerous diseases which abbreviate the lives and effectiveness of men and livestock; illiteracy; tribal, caste, and linguistic divisions; the authority, at least locally, of traditional elites of chieftains and headmen, princes, and sultans; religious practices obstructive of efficiency: these were their inheritance from the colonial period and they have not provided favorable points of departure for the construction of modern societies and polities. The traditional order on the one side and the ill-born fragments of modernity on the other, are so intertwined with each other that it has been extraordinarily difficult to break out of the confinement which they have imposed.

It is quite possible that the traditional culture contains potentialities for modernization that have not been realized. The traditional order has, however, so far offered little that has been helpful to the process of modernization, beyond the stability and recalcitrance to change which have served at least as checks on the emergence of an always threatening chaos. Furthermore, whatever the modern elites of the new states might say on ceremonial occasions, and whatever concessions they might have to make to traditional intellectual-religious elites—as they have done, for example, in Pakistan, Burma and Ceylon, or to traditional political elites, as in Nigeria and Morocco—they are inclined, on the whole, to have little confidence in the traditional order as they perceive it. To them it has been an obstacle rather than an aid to the realization of their goal of modernity.

What are their other resources for the creation of these modern societies? From the colonial regime they have inherited in a few cases, as in the Sudan, India, Ghana, Ceylon.

Malaya and some parts of Nigeria, a civil service ranging from competent to outstanding in quality and already highly indigenized.[3] At the moment of independence, the Asian and English-speaking West African countries inherited a press in the metropolitan language and in the vernacular languages; the former was either foreign-owned and conservative or domestically owned and usually agitational, the latter a pale shadow of their "betters" in the metropolitan language. Only in India was there a large number of professional journals, some important Indian editors of Indian-owned newspapers, and a considerable number of Indian journalists. In Ceylon there were important newspapers under indigenous ownership. In English-speaking West Africa, an indigenous corps of journalists was in existence, whereas in French-speaking Africa, there has been practically no press corps which was qualitatively or numerically worth speaking about. From their pre-independence political history, they brought with them a number of political parties, sometimes—as in India, Burma, and Tanganyika—one of them vastly preponderant together with a motley of tiny minority parties, sometimes—as in Indonesia or Malaya—a variety of more or less equal parties representing particular sectional interests, religious groups, or doctrinal standpoints. Most of these parties, except for the preponderant Congress-type parties, were composed of the personal followers of powerful or outstanding individuals; they were poorly organized, with inadequate funds, and had few reliable full-time workers. The English-speaking parts of Africa inherited a small number of university colleges, usually of respectable standard. In the French-speaking territory of Africa, only one university was inherited and that of very recent creation, but there were several good *lycées*. In the Middle East, there was one good undergraduate college entirely supported from abroad, and several of poorer

3. They were less well provided for in the French-speaking territories and practically not at all in Indonesia and the Belgian Congo.

quality. In South and Southeast Asia, there was a much larger number of mediocre universities and numerous colleges, a few of which were good, most of which were very poor. In Indonesia, there were several professional schools on the verge of being amalgamated into a university, in Singapore a college about to be upgraded to a university, in Ceylon one university, in Pakistan, two undistinguished universities embracing a larger number of colleges. The elementary and secondary school systems which were inherited were even less adequate than the universities for coping with the number of pupils which the aspiration to eliminate illiteracy would soon place upon them. The trade-union movement which was inherited from the colonial period was almost always small—corresponding to the miniscule size of the industrial working class—ill-organized, and primarily political in its intentions and interests. As in the case of the political parties, but more so, their administrative apparatus was meager with very few full-time employees and scanty financial resources. Voluntary associations tended to represent parochial, tribal, and local territorial interests. Civic and reform associations concerned with problems on a national scale were few and weak.

What resources did the political elites of the new states have within themselves to forward the work of modernization? They were among the most educated persons in their societies. Where there were universities and colleges, the political leadership tended to come from the students and graduates of these institutions. Where these were lacking, they came from the high schools. Except for a small number of secondary school and college teachers, who were often cut off from politics by virtue of the foreign sources of their income and the conditions of their service, a large proportion of the highly educated were politically involved. There were small professional classes consisting of lawyers and doctors, the former contributing considerably to the independence movement. Journalism, too, was highly political. The vocational opportunities available to the politically interested among the educated before independence were largely clerical, forensic, and literary. There were few scientists and engineers, few ex-civil servants (politics and the civil service were incompatible), very few business men of much organizational experience. The politicians themselves were not on the whole "machine men." They were agitators rather than organizers.

Except in British India, the political movements of the colonial world were late in getting started. There was nothing of political significance before World War I, in Africa and most of Asia.[4] In Africa, indeed, even the 1920's and 1930's constitute part of the prehistory of the independence movements. Against this background, most of the political elite was bound to be young and inexperienced, inexperienced above all in responsible participation in a parliamentary system. The periods in which they were allowed responsibility for domestic affairs, under the surveillance of the foreign ruler, were few. An "inexperience" of economic organization, of administration, of difficult decision-making was further complicated by the tradition of oppositional politics which the colonial system fostered.

The outlook which had developed among the political activists and their intermittent followers during the pre-independence period was naturally intensely nationalistic. In so far as attention had been given to the condition which would follow independence, something like liberal democracy was generally thought to be prerequisite for the new order of things.[5] Elections, parties, and parliaments were thought of as

4. The professional politicians of the semisovereign states of the Middle East in the period between the two world wars were experienced intriguers and wire-pullers. The full sovereignty of the period following World War II saw these persons almost completely expelled from political life. Their place has been taken by soldiers, lawyers, and journalists.

5. This has become less characteristic of the elites who came to independence and to power in later years. The sight of so many new states collapsing into oligarchy and the changes in metropolitan opinion have made the establishment of liberal democratic regimes appear less compelling. The length and bitterness of the war in Algeria must also have contributed to the intolerance with which that new regime began its career.

essential. Freedom of association and expression, freedoms so often suppressed under foreign rule, were generally expected. Even more central, however, was a fervent belief in, and expectation of, national unity, a total mobilization for social and economic progress. They believed in strong leadership supported by a national consensus.

Traditional indigenous conceptions of the ordering of "public affairs," especially the idea of a community-wide consensus, were more deeply rooted than the political elites believed when they first acceded to power. The institutionalization of dissensus and its protection by a constitutional order did not appear so contradictory to their less acknowledged traditional conceptions because they thought that once independence was won, the consensual unity of the whole people would naturally emerge.[6] But even if unity had existed the elites of the new states would still have encountered difficulty. They wanted to do more than merely reign in a unified and independent nation.

It requires organizational skill to exercise authority successfully over a large territory, to exercise that authority to change institutions, and it requires more than the leadership of a party towards the attainment of power. The agitational skills of opposition, the ascendancy of a charismatic personality over colleagues whose only merits are enthusiasm and dedication to the independence struggle, are not sufficient for the purposes of governing. Governing requires the appreciation of a civil service and the ability to use it. It requires a civil service. And the civil service inheritances of the political elites have differed markedly. The Indian, Malayan, Nigerian, Ceylonese, Sudanese, and the Ghanaian were the

6. They did not foresee that representative institutions and public liberties could produce a dissensus which could threaten them. This was especially true of those political elites which were successful earlier. As time passed, the newer political elites became more skeptical about the constitutional regime and, like the new Algerian government, were ready to undertake an oligarchy from the very beginning. The Algerians were the heirs of a postindependence tradition, new to the politics of the new states.

most fortunate in their inheritance of a considerable body of indigenous, experienced, well-educated, higher civil servants. The Indonesians, the Tanganyikans, and most of the French-speaking African states were much less fortunate. They did not have such a class of indigenous higher civil servants. The quasi-new states of the Arab Middle East, for the most part, fell between these two positions. They had indigenous higher civil servants but their standards were not on a par with some of those who had grown up under British tutelage.

The revenues available to the new elites at the moment of independence were ample for the provision for their own individual and familial needs, to live at a level appropriate to the rulers of a state. They were at the opposite extreme as regards their adequacy for the modernization of their societies.

IV

Life has not turned out as the elites expected at the moment of independence. Their resources did not measure up to their aspirations. The enthusiasm which the fulfilment of their aspirations for independence called forth did not long survive the tasks of organizing and conducting a modern state. The fact that it very soon became the style of the new states to have "development plans" meant that, instead of working piecemeal and solving such problems as they could, they articulated and publicly committed themselves to remote and comprehensive goals. Almost always these goals were in excess of what could be attained, partly because of the temptation, in projecting oneself into the future, to see oneself in a somewhat more elevated and advanced condition than one is likely to be. Quantitative and even qualitative insufficiencies of personnel, terrible shortages of capital, the obduracy of the traditional social structure, have impeded forward movement. The very process of planning with its specifications of requirements made the elites of the new states even more aware of the deficiencies of their resources and accomplishments than they might otherwise have been. The strain came not only from the excess of goals over resources, but also from the internal incompatibility of the goals themselves.

The conflicts among such goals as the improvement of the capital equipment of the economy, the enhancement of the symbolic grandeur of the society, the creation of national unity, the furtherance of an indigenous modern culture, and the operation of a set of modern political institutions aggravated dissensions within their societies. Instead of forcing them to reconcile themselves to a policy of adapting the various goals to their limited resources, it simply heightened their anguish to perceive these *economic* scarcities in the most painful sense of the word, a sense which had never dawned on them previously.

Failure weakens self-confidence and self-esteem, and it arouses criticism of persons, practices, and institutions. This has happened in every new state. Their failure to realize aspirations which have been so integral to their conception of their own dignity has heightened the elites' sensitivity to criticism. This sensitivity is especially pronounced because of their sense of identity with the state and their relative immunity from criticism by fellow-countrymen during the last period of the independence struggle when conflicts among various sectors of the anticolonial elites were hidden from the public view. Criticism by the colonial ruler and by the organs of opinion affiliated with the colonial ruler was expected, in fact, was accepted as establishing the legitimacy of their leadership. But criticism by their fellow-countrymen and criticism by comrades-in-arms was a relatively new experience, at least in the degree of intensity and publicity in which it has been carried on after independence and until, as has happened in so many new states, it has been suppressed.

Of all the kinds of criticism which these faltering movements have generated, the criticism of institutions has been most readily accepted. The incumbent elites could relatively easily dissociate themselves from institutions which are based on foreign models. Indeed, one of the ways in which the elites have sought to diminish the impact of criticism directed against their own performance has been to displace criticism on to the institutions through which they had tried to work and failed (e.g., Indonesia and Ceylon).

Economic development had, of course, been taken for granted by the nationalist contenders for their countries' independence. On the whole, however, very little thought was given to it. It was taken for granted that once the foreign exploiter had been removed from their backs, the natural wealth of their countries would accrue to their own people. The socialistic bent of so many of the members of the elites made them envisage a greater prosperity after independence once a more or less socialistic regime had been established.

Economic development as a major concern came rather late on the scene. It was probably not entirely a creation of the elites of the new states but rather a creation of professional economists, the United Nations, and the British and French colonial offices preparing to set their charges free in the best possible condition and to avert the criticism of anti-imperialists in the advanced states. The Indian experience also had a part in the process.

However that may be, when economic development did emerge as a major concern, it pushed out of the way other, older concerns which were more superficially rooted in the outlook of the elites. The slowness of economic development could be attributed to those uncomfortably fitting, embarrassing institutions which fostered and permitted criticism and exposed shortcomings, sometimes truthfully and sometimes less than truthfully. The slowness was inevitable and the elevation of economic development into the status of a major criterion of the world's judgment of any particular country naturally aggravated the strain which already existed between the political elites and the institutional system which they were trying to operate.

No less injurious than the frustration of aspirations for economic progress has been the frustration of expectations concerning internal unity. India's, Malaya's, and Burma's misfortunes at the very beginning were not only extreme, they also sobered the expectations of their elites and made them less confident of complete unity. In other countries, disunity came later—sometimes promoted by the policy of the government—and when it came, its effect was traumatic and, as in Ceylon and Ghana, occasionally more traumatic than reality justified. On the whole, progress towards unity has been slow. The new states have in many cases threatened to disintegrate into the constituent tribal and communal elements of which they are still predominantly composed.[7] The fears have been aggravated by the civil wars and riots in other new states.

Part of the hostility of the modern elites against the traditional elites of their own countries arises from their fear that the survival of chiefs and sultans will not only hold up the progress of their societies but will actually tear them apart. Traditional parochial jealousies, given contemporary political form and covered by the names of "political parties," present a constant menace of disintegration. The difficulty is compounded by the fact that in most of the new states, the sense of national identity is a creation of the still living, still ruling generation and is only very faintly alive in other sections of the population. Like so many new beliefs fervently expressed, it is a tenuously poised phenomenon which requires constant reaffirmation for its support and feels endangered by the perception of its denial.

India is the only new state where the sense of national identity goes back for as many as three generations. India had a

7. Indonesia, Burma, Malaya, Ceylon, India, Pakistan, Sudan, Iraq, Jordan, Lebanon, Ghana, Nigeria, Congo, the Republic of the Congo, have all experienced civil disorder arising from traditional tribal, communal, religious, linguistic, and ethnic cleavages.

modern foreign ruler ruling over most of its territory longer than almost any other new state. This helped it to define its image. As a result, at least the educated class acquired a sense of its collective existence as a country. The Indian elite with all its regional, caste, and communal loyalties, is relatively confident of its Indian nature. In India, as elsewhere, parts of the elite feel uneasy about whether they are sufficiently indigenous, but there is less of this feeling in India than in any other new state. In India, too, even the more secure elite worries about the fissiparousness of Indian society. How much more worried must be those elites who are themselves newer to their nationality and whose fellow citizens are even more strange to the consciousness of themselves as citizens of a single country. Against this background it is easy to see why the elites feel that criticism of their actions is both evidence of, and a stimulus to, the breaking apart of the frail political order.[8]

V

The desire to be respected in the world, to have their states and themselves respected, is one of the great aims of the elites of the new states. The new states are now sovereign, but they are not independent. Their economic dependence is visible and distressing to them; their intellectual dependence is not so generally acknowledged and not so distressingly experienced. Their dependence on the favorable opinion of the outer world is often vehemently denied but remains nonthe-

8. Quite apart from genuine attachments to their own particularistic communities, which can coexist with a genuine attachment to the idea of a comprehensive nationality, many members of the political elites cannot resist the temptation to exploit existing intercommunal hostilities for short-term political purposes. It is so difficult to accomplish something substantial in the fields of economic and social development that symbolic accomplishments such as obtaining precedence for a particular ethnic or linguistic group are rendered especially attractive. Much of the development in Ceylon preceding the Emergency of 1958 is to be accounted for by the greater ease of symbolic accomplishments. The result is to aggravate what is already feared.

less a powerful motive. They wish to cut a figure and to play a part. To be entitled to do so they must stand for something. They do not believe that their wounds alone—the wounds of colonial subjugation—are a sufficient qualification for the world's respect. Accomplishment that the world respects and the legitimacy of their representativeness are felt to be necessary to lay claim to the respectful attention of the great world of the advanced countries and to the leadership of the underdeveloped ones.

Neither of these can be confidently claimed if one is a failure at home and if one's failure is being proclaimed in press and parliament. The constitutional system of representative government and public liberties provides for such liberties of criticism. It is, therefore, a drag on the aspiration to be noticed and appreciated outside the boundaries of one's own country. Of course, those who are hypersensitive in such matters, as the political elites of the new states often are, will exaggerate the extent to which the outer world notices the criticism to which they are subjected at home. But hypersensitivity to criticism is characteristic of these new elites, and in their efforts to put forward the most impressive image of the state and the progress of their countries, they experience criticism as a betrayal. It is regarded as a disclosure to the world that the country is not modernizing itself as it should. It weakens the position of the country in its striving to make an impression.

So, the strains of reality break the constellation of goals which appeared, at the moment of independence, to be internally consistent and even mutually reinforcing. Constitutional government seemed at first to be not only compatible with international respect but also conducive to it. Now it seems to stand in its way. Economic progress has become more precious than constitutional government in the eyes of the world. When constitutional government reveals deficiencies in economic development, it undermines its own support.

Note on the impact of metropolitan opinion concerning the primacy of economic development and the inappropriateness of constitutional government

Opinion in the advanced countries has probably contributed to this rearrangement of the value pattern of the elites of the new states. More and more, intellectual opinion in the West has come to regard constitutional government in the new states as a lost cause and even as a cause well lost. It has come to regard constitutional government as inevitably doomed to deterioration and disappearance, given the handicaps it confronts. It has, however, gone further than the mere confrontation of the obstacles to constitutional government. It has gone so far as to argue that the tasks of economic and social development taken upon themselves by the elites of the new states cannot be adequately performed and are even hindered by the machinery of representative institutions and public liberties. Distinguished Western economists who are all in favor of constitutional government in their own countries have provided a legitimation for the suppression of constitutional government in some of the new states.

The Soviet and Chinese models, either directly perceived by the political elites of the new states or perceived by the medium of British, French, and American writers, have provided the same sort of influential legitimation for the suppression of constitutional government in the name of economic development.

Western intellectual opinion, out of compassion and contempt, has helped further the process. The proposition that the new states should find a mode of government more congenial to their traditions than the imported systems with which they began their sovereign careers is an encouragement to discard constitutional government. (Not that much encouragement has been needed!)

VI

There is some truth in the contention that the native genius does not find its best expression in the system of constitutional government. The traditional cast of mind which the elites of the new states so often bear within them under the surface of their consciousness has no place within it for dissent and criticism. In traditional cultures, conflicts are settled by an emergent consensus rather than by voting. Continuous criticism and institutionalized dissent have no place in an order in which consensus, once attained, is expected to dissolve differences and to leave no enduring lines of cleavage.

The authorities of lineages and villages—primordial and traditional authorities—are not congenial to the specification and delimitation of powers. The powers of chief headman are, according to the traditional view, diffuse. They are, of course, limited by traditional obligations, as well as by considerations of prudence, but the ruler is not bound by enacted laws, written constitutions, or recorded and binding precedents.

Despite their differences, traditional and primordial authority have much in common with charismatic authority. The charismatic conception of authority—their own and that of the heroes of the independence struggle who became the first rulers of the new states—has left a deep imprint on the minds of their present elites. Beliefs as to the proper mode of action of authorities who were formed in the traditional sectors of the society and in the independence movement—the beliefs which the political elites of the new states inherit—are not congenial to the restraints of parliamentary procedure, of independent judiciaries, and tough-minded, strong-willed civil services.

The traditional image of "public life" moreover has no room for *legislation* and for the public discussion preparatory to a compromise among conflicting contentions. Laws are not *made* in traditional societies. They are *found* in judgments made in the resolution of particular disputes. Debates in parliament and decisions by majorities, frequently composed of very heterogeneous interests, although having certain parallels in tribal discussions about succession, have no parallels in the major functions of policy-formation and law-making. The rudimentary governmental apparatus of traditional societies is not oriented toward the making of laws or their implementation. It is oriented toward the maintenance of order by the enunciation of what is right. It does not seek to do new things, things which have never been done before. It does not promulgate new laws. Above all, it does not promulgate new laws to establish new social and economic arrangements. It is a mode of affirming established rules.

Parliamentary institutions, law-making mechanisms, and the cognate institutions of press and parties are therefore foreign elements, alien to the traditional image of the world of public decisions. They do not seem "natural." The political elites have to use a procedure with which they do not feel at ease; they must do things which do not fall into the pattern of authority and action as it is understood by themselves and their fellow-countrymen. The political elites of the new states certainly do not wish to go back to their traditional and tribal societies where leaders, once established, were more secure in their status and tenure. Parliaments, insofar as they are not transformed into a system of "guided democracy" which avoids the discomforts of parliamentary democracy, are constantly voting on measures put forward by the government. Even where the government's majority is secure, the incumbent elite is constantly being forced to undergo scrutiny and to seek approval anew. They have to listen to their policies and themselves being discussed and criticized, often rather acrimoniously.

They are confronted, too, not only by criticism of their past performances but by the refusal of parliament and public opinion to allow rulers to do whatever they wish in the future. The situation of rulers is not made more agreeable by the fact that the oppositional elites tend to regard parliamentary discussion primarily as a means of denouncing and embarrassing their opponents; this is exaggerated by the tendency on the part of those in opposition to regard those they criticize as aliens—an attitude derived from the pattern of criticism of colonial rulers when the rulers were genuinely alien.

This is not the way things worked according to the traditional image of government. Rulers had to be selected when the previous incumbent died or was killed and this might be done by a consensual election by those qualified by age, eminence, and kinship to make the decision. But once elected or acceded, the ruler was generally not subjected to constant scrutiny in an *institutionalized* way. The difficulties of carrying out their policies and the feeling of vulnerability before criticism because of their failures and difficulties make them especially fearful of displacement.

Elite anxiety about displacement is not the normal state of affairs in traditional societies. Their heirs among the incumbent elites are uneasy in the presence of this novel possibility. Since criticism implies the possibility of displacement, in addition to the other damages which it can inflict, the incumbent rulers naturally tend to resent bitterly their critics in the opposition. This bitterness is not reduced by the fact that many of the critics are former colleagues, classmates, and friends. All this appearance and reality of obstruction from allies and opponents irritates the governing politicians and makes them wish to curb it. It also discredits the system among those sections who on one level of consciousness accept parliamentary institutions and on another reject it, but who in either case wish from their rulers the air and evidence of effectiveness. "Talk," against the background of stagnation on the one side and the high expectations of the fruits of independence on the other, weakens their acceptance of parliamentary politics and makes them ready to accept a regime which asserts that it "means business." Oligarchy, in most new states has at least mastered the terminology of "dynamism." This gives it an advantage.

VII

The charismatic is as much the enemy of constitutional government as the primordial and the traditional. The charismatic stands at the acknowledged center of the modern politics of the new states. The causes are various. In part, it is an inheritance from the necessities of the independence struggle which, however brief, required strong personalities capable of withstanding the threats of rulers and rivals and of imposing their ascendancy on a widening circle of followers; it could not have emerged or persisted without them. The nature of the struggle tended to bring to the forefront persons who were capable of detaching themselves, to some extent and for the time being, from the connections of kinship and locality in the traditional sector of society and from the obligations of occupation or profession in the modern sector. The capacity for the former and the latter kinds of detachment is found in personalities of a force which cannot be contained by institutions—this is what we designate as charisma—and it calls to those in whom a parallel disposition is to be observed. It is found especially among the youthful who are in revolt against the primordial, the traditional, and the civil.

Responsiveness to this transcendence of institutions is culturally sustained in the societies of the great world religions of Hinduism, Islam, and Buddhism. All of these great creeds preach the moral supremacy of the saint, selfless and detached from earthly ties and from the impulsions of the physical organism, freed from egotism in every regard. Earthly authority, too, is expected to bear some of this sanctity. Those who grow up in these cultures retain some of the fundamental patterns of response derived from their religious origins. In the areas of the world less impregnated with the great world religions, the charismatic expectation manifests itself without the deeper cultural support, but it manifests itself, nonetheless. In Africa, too, there is responsiveness to charismatic authority. The independence movements there threw up the same kinds of leaders and attracted the same kinds of followers. The absence of the influence of the great world religions of Asia and the Middle East was compensated by the greater impulsion, in Africa, towards individual charisma as a result of the greater disjunction between the modern and the traditional institutional systems.

All this works against the parliamentary system, with its debates, bargaining, compromise, and voting by majorities. From the heroic standpoint, party and parliamentary politics is seen to be very egotistical, very preoccupied with mundane and even base interests. The responsiveness to charismatic personalities and the belief in the possibility and goodness of a spontaneous consensus go together to form a "natural Rousseauism." The notion of parliament as a means of accommodating conflicting interests and conflicting ideas of the common good does not fit a view of politics which regards interests narrower than those of the whole society as having no legitimacy and which regards the conflict of ideas of the common good as meaningless. Rousseauism and constitutional parliamentary government do not go well together.

VIII

The idea of a consensual society, safe from the contamination of individual and parochial egotism, has its deeper roots in the traditional view of the rightful dominion of saintly or sagacious elders and the earlier self-isolation of the independence movement. Among modern sources, it receives power from the idea of modern socialism, adapted to the situation of an underdeveloped, newly sovereign state.

It would be wrong to think of the political elites of the new states as Marxist or Communist. The Marxist or Communist image of the right political order seems an afterthought rather than an actively impelling model of the right governmental procedures. There are very few real Communists or wholehearted Marxists in dominant positions in African politics. There are not many more in South and Southeast Asia despite the longer exposure to Communist ideas and the importance of the Russian Revolution for the Asian nationalist movements and the recent influence of Chinese communism. The Soviet model is seen vaguely as socialist and progressive. The idea of a totalitarian dictatorship is repugnant to most Asian and African politicians—even though they might in reality practice an approximation of it. It embodies a belief in the goodness of a highly centralized, ruthlessly decisive authority which is uncongenial to their general beliefs and even their personal dispositions towards an emanative and exhortative consensus. Nonetheless, there are few of them who are not socialists of one sort or another.

The socialist ideals of the elites of the new states have many sources. Most obviously and perhaps most superficially the socialist ideal of the African and Asian political elites ever since World War I were formed through their contact with European—primarily French and British—intellectuals. Some variant of socialism was the prevalent political ideal of the European intelligentsia of that period. It was probably their anti-imperialistic attitude that made them the chosen comrades of the Asians and the Africans who studied in Europe from the twenties to the fifties in the present century. The Soviet Union was anti-French and anti-British; it was anti-imperialist and its socialism therefore commended itself. In socialist and communist circles in Europe, Asian and later African students found a welcome which they did not generally find elsewhere in the metropolitan societies.

African and Asian socialism is also to an important extent simply a belief in the superiority of governmental authority to any other form of authority. Coming from, or forming the educated classes of, their own societies whose chief source of stable and remunerative employment, then as now, was government, they tended to attribute high prestige to the civil service. Businessmen were nearly always aliens—in Asia, Europeans, Asians from other Asian countries, or from particular castes; in Africa, Europeans, Asians, Middle Easterners, or from other tribes. The businessman, even in Nigeria, is some distance behind the civil servant.

A strong ruler, backed by a unitary social will and working for the progress of his society, is more pleasing to contemplate than is a society in which progress arises from private vice or from action motivated by the prospect of individual gain. Much of the socialism of the new states is really a declaration of faith in the superiority of the apolitical civil servant over the businessman and the parliamentary and party politician.

The urgency of progress, the intolerability of delay in keeping up, if not closing, the gap which separates the new states from the advanced countries, is an argument for strong, more or less socialistic, government. The socialistic ideal is the ideal of a common goal consensually affirmed. It involves the transcendence of particularistic interests; it assumes the unchallenged acceptance of responsibility for the common good by the government. It therefore renders superfluous the struggle of conflicting interests. A government which is held back by discussion, which is seen as no more than a frustrating obstruction on behalf of private interests, has little to recommend itself to those whose ideal is consensual and "dynamic."

Such beliefs intensify criticism of the parliamentary system which acknowledges a pluralism that is inharmonious with an outlook that is a compound of dynamism and traditionalism. They encourage the critics who would displace the system, weaken the attachments of incumbent politicians to constitutional government, and encourage them to pursue an already sufficiently attractive path away from parliamentary democracy that makes itself offensive by its plurality of viewpoints and the restraint and criticism which these imply.

IX

The intrusion of the military into politics is only one manifestation of this widespread readiness of significant sections

of the educated elite to suspend the system of a self-restrain-
ing government and to replace it by one which affects the air
of strength and a unitary purposefulness. It is not the military but civilian politicians who have promulgated severe
preventive detention laws in Tanganyika and Ghana and
who would like to do so in Nigeria. It is civilian politicians
who have retained on the statute books of Burma, Malaya,
and India the preventive detention laws of the colonial ruler.
Civilians have established "guided democracy" in Indonesia
and have aimed to nationalize newspapers in Ceylon. Civilians have abolished all but one party in Algeria. It is not the
military which guides Tunisia with such a firm hand.
Throughout French-speaking Africa, south of the Sahara,
the one-party state is the creation of civilians. And in most
countries where the military has intervened in politics and
taken over the conduct of government, their action has been
applauded at least for a time by a considerable section of the
politically interested public. Sometimes, as in the Sudan, the
civilian politicians have connived in the instigation of the
military coup. Throughout the Middle East, the military oli-
garchs have found willing collaborators among the politicians.

The fact is that government by the military in some respects brings to a more open expression certain of the political aspirations of those they displace and of those over whom
they exercise power. The military are, in fact, much like the
civilian politicians and the political public. They have a
relatively advanced modern education. They believe in consensual order under the firm guidance of strong leadership—
only more so. They are nationalistic. They too regard themselves as the custodians of modernity. They also have little
respect for those who pursue private interest—although having had less contact with them, the military has also less
experience of compromise with them. The difference is that
many of the members of the civilian elite are more democratic and more populistic, and they derive a substantial part
of their intellectual equipment from Western socialism and

liberalism with which the military has had little to do. Then, too, the political program of the civilian elites before independence, the very mode of organization as a party, committed them to participation in representative assemblies without much thought on the matter. As the victims of executive government under the colonial regime, they formed some attachment to the idea of the practice of public liberties.

The military, which was created in the independence struggle as in Algeria or in opposition to the Japanese as in Burma and Indonesia, carries forward certain of the loose cluster of ideals of the civilian political elite, particularly those which are alien to constitutional government.[9] The weakness of the proponents of constitutional government strengthens such tendencies in the military. In other countries, where the military does not have such experience, the military culture as such has political potentialities. The conception of an authoritatively disciplined social order shares with the preference for emergent consensus a disapproval of sectional interests and institutionalized criticism.

X

All politicians are preoccupied with remaining in power and the danger of being turned out. The politicians of the new states also have this need and they are not yet wedded to the rules which permit opposition and which govern succession. The rules of opposition and succession which are characteristic of constitutional government are not "their rules"; they tend therefore to dissociate themselves from the burden with which they have been saddled, which threatens them with

9. The Indian Army brought up in the British tradition of respect for the ascendancy of the civil arm has had the moral advantage of working with a civilian political elite more tenaciously committed to constitutional government than any in Asia and Africa. Pakistan, however, provides the evidence that the tradition of subordination to the civil arm cannot withstand the sight of an ineffective political elite nominally devoted to constitutional government.

censure and removal. They fall in readily with the criticism of an alien governmental system which they operate with such difficulty and with such problematical results. A passionately impelled cultural revivalism generates an atmosphere which legitimates the suspension or modification of the pattern of political values which they inherited from their colonial rulers and the metropolitan culture.

Constitutional democracy in nearly all of the new states is an alien phenomenon. It is not just that it is different in much of its particular content and in some of its fundamental values from the indigenous tradition, although that itself is a sufficient burden. What concerns us here is that it is experienced as alien by its practitioners and this places them at a disadvantage where indigenous things are at a premium. The elites of the new states are, of course, different from the mass of the population as they are, indeed, in any state. They are different, however, in a significant way by virtue of the cultural disjunction between themselves and their people. This makes, as we have said before, for impatience, but it also makes for a desire to make oneself more indigenous. Awareness of the decayed or rudimentary condition of their indigenous cultural inheritance has made men feel the need to revive it; it has made them feel the need to affirm its value and to deny derogations whether explicit or implicit. In an atmosphere of sensitive nationalism where the dangers to the institutions which have arisen from this still fragile and scantily diffused sense of nationality are real, symbolic affronts to the need to be "of the people," to be authentically indigenous are tangibly felt. The accusation of being a "black Englishman" or a "brown Sahib" is often heard. Even the most Westernized direct it against themselves. The accusation is even more frequently made by those of the political elite who are less educated against those who are more educated; it is a common coin of the currency of demagoguery. The proponents of "alien" institutions feel themselves vulnerable to accusations that they are the defenders of "alien" practices. This diminishes their self-confidence and their attachment to this damning association.

Since it is the tradition of self-limiting representative government and of pluralistic public liberties which is "alien," and since it is the tradition of diffuse charismatic authority and of an uninstitutionalized consensus which is indigenous, constitutional government tends naturally to be the loser in such a confrontation. The difficulty of actually governing societies which are not easily governable, of arousing a real, rather than a fictitious, consensus from the midst of deep diversity, of generating dynamism in the midst of a distrustful adherence to tradition would impel an elite suffering from a sense of frustration to be impatient with obstacles. The complex value pattern of the elites of the new states— directed as it is towards so many divergent goals which were so delicately equilibrated with each other—is difficult to sustain. The charge of being "alien" and the belief that one is "alien" in one's practice is an additional strain on the value pattern. The strain is resolved by movement away from constitutional government.

XI

Yet with all these handicaps, constitutional government has shown a certain obstinate capacity for survival in the new states. Where it has gone down, it has not gone down without an effort to save it or, at least, some pretense of its retention. It has not sunk its roots deeply enough to guarantee its survival as a whole in all the new states. It has, however, gone deeply enough to force those who destroy it to pay it some of the compliments which vice pays to virtue.

There are, moreover, countries in which it has survived in quite integral form. India, Sierra Leone, and Malaya have thus far managed, since the attainment of independence, to avoid the prolonged or extensive suspensions of constitutional government which have happened elsewhere. Succession has been practiced according to the law. Elections have been held, parties other than the government party are allowed to operate, and some freedom of discussion has been maintained, even if not perfectly. The courts have functioned well and institutions have been permitted a fair degree of autonomy. Of course, Malaya and Sierra Leone have been sovereign for a much shorter time than India; many states which became independent later have, however, proceeded with little delay towards oligarchy. The closer adherence of Malaya and Sierre Leone to constitutional government is not accidental.

To take India first. It is the oldest of the new states and the largest. Its record is not unblemished but it compares favorably with more advanced countries in its maintenance of a constitutional order. Its achievement is exceptionally impressive when one considers the numerous difficulties which the government of India has had to deal with since its origin: the very size of the country and its population, the chaotic conditions of its establishment including the integration of the princely states, the assassination of its founder, the inundation of refugees, the persisting poverty of the people, and their religious, linguistic and caste separation from each other. Few new states could draw up a more depressing list of obstacles to constitutional government. Yet India was and remains a liberal democracy. The press is free to criticize, elections are held regularly and are relatively free from corruption. Civic associations are free to agitate on behalf of their programs. Universities, despite financial dependence, are not dominated by the government as regards the content of what they teach. The government is restrained and the courts are vigilant in the protection of the rights of the vast majority of the government critics. (Only in connection with Kashmir and during the Chinese border crisis has the Indian government deviated from its good record.) Finally, the Indian army has stayed away from politics.

The explanation for its success seems to lie in the characteristics of its political and intellectual elites. The Indian elite has the longest experience of politics and of administration. In its beginnings it was thoroughly liberal, and even though the liberal leadership of the nationalist movement was in time supplanted by a more populistic leadership, which placed more weight on indigenous traditions and institutions than had the liberals, their influence did not die out. The Indian liberals were never overcome. They were merely supplanted and their ideas were assimilated into something else. They never discredited themselves by corruption or incompetence or by the devious combinations of party politics. Their good name survived their power in the movement, and with their name, there also persisted respect for their outlook and the kinds of political institutions which they favored. This liberal influence was manifested most notably in the Indian constitution.

The liberal constitutionalist phase was present in most of the nationalist movements of Asia and Africa. But its eminent figures were fewer in number in Africa than they were in India, and in the Middle Eastern countries they became discredited through involvement in the practices and malpractices of parliamentary politics of incompletely sovereign countries.

British rule in India lasted long enough and its cultural and educational penetration was deep enough to create, even among the majority of those who wished the British to leave and who were not uncritically pro-Western, a genuine appreciation of British institutions as well as much of British practice in India. The same could not be said for most of the rest of Asia, Africa, or the Middle East where the European impact was too brief and too superficial in its penetration. (The attachment of the educated French-speaking African to

French culture is very deep, but it is more confined to very
small numbers, to cultural and intellectual matters, and to—
often illiberal—political *doctrines;* it does not ordinarily extend to political and governmental *institutions.*)

Indian colleges and universities have often been criticized,
and often justly. They are numerous, and no more than a
small proportion of them are good and only a few are excellent. From among their vast numbers of students, however,
they have produced many highly qualified graduates, attached to modern liberal culture and with an effective mas-
tery of its substance. Indians have gone overseas to study—
until recently largely to Great Britain—for a longer time and
in larger numbers than the citizens of any other colonial territory or new state. Modern British liberal culture, especially
its liberal political culture (including British socialism which
is largely liberal and constitutionalist) has thus found a large
and firmly fixed assimilation in India. This has furnished the
matrix of opinion within which Indian political life has been
conducted.

In addition to this relatively congenial intellectual environment—much more congenial to constitutional government
than that enjoyed by any other new state—Indian political
life has enjoyed a number of other advantages. For one thing,
the Indian constitution as a federal constitution has corre-
sponded closely enough to the realities of Indian political and
cultural diversity to enable it to withstand the successful pressure for the modification of state boundaries. Furthermore,
the decentralization of authority to the state governments has
checked the pressure for centralization, mobilization, and so
many of the other manifestations of "dynamism" known all
too well in most of the other new states. The federal constitution has given influence to state politicians whose indigenous
culture was unquestionable and who could not be called
"brown Englishmen." They had the self-confidence of the
genuine article and yet the federal constitution forced them to

collaborate with the leadership at the center which was more closely allied with the liberal traditions and culture that bore them. The numerous links between State and Union government avoid a sharp disjunction between the indigenous and the alien which troubles other new states and at the same time links the periphery of the society to its modern center. India is forced into the give-and-take of pluralistic politics by its federal structure. Professional politicians, who have succeeded in making it work, have thus acquired a vested interest in the maintenance of the system.

India has, moreover, developed a large class of lawyers who have acquired a vested interest in the Indian judicial system, in court procedure, in arguing from precedent, etc. The judicial system, too, whatever its defects, has a long history and reputation for justice, particularly at higher levels. The good name of British magistrates and judges has carried over to their Indian successors. This also contributes to the stability of the constitutional system. Justice is kept relatively free from politics. The rule of the law has become a value to judges and to lawyers.

Indian journalism—again less good than it ought to be—has developed a large corps of journalists, editors, and publishers with an austere conception of the role of the press and a vested interest in the freedom of the press to criticize and to remain free of governmental control. Of course, the Indian press is not very well placed financially; it does not have enough revenue from advertising, and parts of it are too dependent on government announcements for news and income. Still, it is concerned with its place in Indian public life and it is also a large enough activity to become a vested economic interest of its owners who do not wish it to be interfered with. Although in some cases this is injurious to the internal integrity of the press, it serves as a bulwark against external interference. Indian politicians and administration, despite occasional departures, have accepted the independence of the press and its right to criticize.

The large Indian educated class offers another support to Indian constitutional order through those of its members who formed the Indian Civil Service and who are its successors, the Indian Administrative Service. This *corps d'èlite*, by its high skill, its self-confidence and prestige, provides the Indian politician with an instrument which protects the system from the inevitability of failure and therewith from the loss of confidence which accompanies every failing system.

In India, too, there is a strong countercurrent of belief in consensual politics, in finding a truly "Indian" way of conducting political life. Again, there are those who demand a "dynamic mobilization," and who think that party politics and parliamentary politics represent costly, ill-working importations.[10] The reputation of professional politicians among a large proportion of Indian intellectuals is low.[11] The obloquy which would inevitably accrue to the politicians from a greater degree of failure—were a competent civil service lacking—would greatly damage the already weak position of the Indian politician in public opinion and would heighten the demand for their replacement by a pattern more in consonance with the conception of politics prevailing throughout much of the "third world."

The pressure for traditionalization has been withstood by a more fortunate relationship between the traditional and modern elites. The traditional elite of maharajahs has been set aside, but one part of another traditional elite, the Brahmins, has been in the process of self-modernization for nearly one hundred years. Furthermore, a third section of the Indian

10. The exertions of Jayaprakash Narayan as expressed in his essay *Towards the Reconstruction of the Indian Polity* are among the many evidences of this yearning in India. Yet the critical response to the scheme put forward by this revered personality is evidence of the fading of utopian consensualism from Indian political opinion.
11. The political alienation of a large part of the Indian intellectual class is a handicap to Indian democracy and it could become a danger. We have the impression, however, that the unrealistic and carping attitude of Indian intellectuals—especially among journalists and college and university teachers —is diminishing. Their criticism seems to be becoming more differentiated because their expectations are becoming more realistic.

elite, the local Congress politicians, has been sufficiently modernized while remaining in many important respects a *dhotiwallah* class. Thus India has not had the disjunction between traditional elites and modern elites which has existed in Ceylon, Burma, Pakistan, Indonesia, Ghana, and South Viet-Nam. In this way, the pluralistic structure of modern Indian political society is supported by its own modern traditions and by the autonomous attachments of several professions integral to the public life of a constitutional society.

The situation of Sierra Leone is rather different from India in many important respects. The population is less than one one-hundredth of India's. Its independence is very recent and its independence movement only a little less so. In some respects, however, the similarity to India is striking. Sierra Leone has an advanced educational system which has trained a small modern elite. Fourah Bay College—now the University College of Sierra Leone—is the oldest modern university in Africa. It is an institution which for many decades was the major seedbed of the educated men who formed the first, now vanquished, generation of constitutional liberal nationalists of Africa. The Creole population of Sierra Leone has a longer and more intense exposure to European cultural influence than any important part of African society. The Creole population produced, through Fourah Bay, a small class of lawyers, doctors, teachers, and journalists who were proud of their calling and who felt the need to live up to the responsibilities of their status in society. Thus there existed several of the conditions necessary for a constitutional regime—a long modern tradition, an effective system of higher education and a self-esteeming professional class. A sufficient number of the traditional elite has existed intact in the Protectorate; their offspring who have obtained higher education have done so in an atmosphere which did not set them in extreme conflict with either their forebears or the modern educated elite of Freetown.

In Malaya, the traditional elite has remained in the saddle, not as a traditional elite as in Saudi Arabia, but in a modernized self-transformation. The Malayan elite has thereby been able to avoid that sharp cleavage between the surviving traditional elites of chiefs, mullahs, and monks which has driven the latter, as in Ghana and in South Viet-Nam, into a defensive aggressiveness. This has given it a considerable advantage over many new states.

Malaya had suffered from a long period of revolutionary guerrilla warfare before the attainment of independence. Such disorder existed in Burma, too, but there it has never been effectively put down and its continuation has weakened the prestige of the government. In Malaya the suppression, which was the work of the colonial government, was successfully executed. The Malayan political elite associated itself, as far as public opinion was concerned, with this successful campaign against the guerrillas. It thereby gained the credit which strength confers, as well as the credit which came from its willingness to end the emergency and to forgive the rebels.

The Malayan government thus seemed both strong and magnanimous. In addition to this, it has not since independence staked its reputation on grandiose economic achievements. This has saved it from embarrassing failure and from a reduction in its public esteem. Its federal structure is another advantage. Malaya has, however, a business class which conforms with the classical Asian model of being ethnically alien. It has the usual linguistic problems of new states; it is ethnically heterogeneous and it has recently taken on the additional burdens entailed by the transformation of Malaya into Malaysia.

Thus, moderation and matter-of-factness in its political elite, a relative freedom from tension in its relations with its indigenous culture, a more or less harmonious collaboration of the economic and political elites, and an effective administration coupled with a minimal degree of separatist sentiment

in the country have helped to keep Malaya within the framework of constitutional government. Threatening this framework is the deep ethnic cleavage, made more pronounced by
the accession of Singapore, Sarawak, and North Borneo and
the menace of military involvement with Indonesia. Israel, in
an ecologically and ethnically less difficult situation, has managed to retain its constitutional form of government. Malaysia
might be able to do the same.

Israel, too, is a new state which has, thus far, been able to
withstand the pressures which have overcome constitutional
government in other countries. Like Algeria, but with a very
different aftermath, Israel was born from a victorious war; it
has ever since lived in an approximate state of siege. It had to
create the machinery of government. It has its problems of
cultural heterogeneity; it lives under the strain of striving
for economic development. In these respects it resembles
other new states where constitutional government has badly
faltered.

Israel's success in avoiding that outcome may be attributed
to a number of factors which are unique among the new
states. Whereas in other states the idea of nationality is yet to
be inculcated effectively into large parts of the population,
the external and voluntary recruitment of the Jewish population of Palestine and Israel has meant that there was already
some common conception of a collective self among the strata
of the population which formed the framework of the society.[12] The influx of the exiles and victims of National Socialism brought to Palestine and to Israel persons whose Jewish identity had been underscored by their misfortunes. The
recruitment of Asian and North African Jews after the establishment of the State of Israel introduced culturally diverse
peoples who nonetheless regarded themselves as Jews above

12. The Israeli Arabs are at present so restricted in their rights and powers
that they may be regarded as politically negligible vis-à-vis the vastly preponderant Jewish population.

all else. Furthermore, by the time these "Oriental" Jews came to supplement Jews of central and western European derivation, the latter had already set the pattern and occupied the key positions of the society into which the newcomers had to fit. Israeli politics, although strongly socialistic, are not on the whole populistic. The greater recentness of arrival of the least educated and least modern meant that politicians in Israel have been on the whole free from the pressure to placate the deity of a tradition with which they are out of sympathy and the simplest elements of the populace which worships that tradition. Furthermore, the modern secular outlook of the Israeli political and cultural elite and the fact that the orthodox Jews cannot effectively claim to be the genuine heirs of the Jewish idea in a way which would put the modernists on the defensive also eases the situation of the Israeli elite.[13] The discipline and morale of the Israeli army have turned compulsory military service into a civil asset by assimilating the culturally peripheral newcomers into the dominant culture.

The high educational level of the Israeli population and a widespread political and civic interest have both made for sufficient diversity of organizational and professional loyalties in a relatively large political elite. Journalism and the law, which are two of the main bulwarks of constitutional government, are both beneficiaries of the advanced modern culture of Israel. Civic and economic associations both attest to and foster the wide dispersion of political sensitivity and concern for the shape of the whole society.

Although Israel is in its particular form unique among the new states, its attachment to constitutional government permits a few hypotheses of general relevance to be enunciated.

13. The orthodox eastern European Jewish rabbinate might from time to time create a disturbance in Israel, but their performance is unlikely to evoke in the Israeli populace the responsiveness which the *ulama* in Pakistan or the Buddhist monks in Burma, South Viet-Nam, or Ceylon have been able to arouse.

One points to the fact that an absence of significant tension between the traditional and the modern elites is one precondition for the maintenance of constitutional government. Another hypothesis points to the more general factors of self-confidence and strength of conviction of the civilian political elite regarding its own cultural and civil legitimacy in the face of the traditional and the military elites. This, in turn, is related to the hypothesis that where the civilian political elite, working within a constitutional system, believes in the genuineness of its own achievement, it will not feel impelled to jettison the system or to abdicate before those who would do so.

XII

What then are the prospects of constitutional government in the new states of Asia and Africa in the remaining third of this century? Will there be an increase in the demand for individual and corporate freedom? Will there emerge a greater respect for a modern form of legal order and a greater readiness to acknowledge the rights conferred by citizenship?

The wider diffusion of a sense of nationality to the point where the territorial boundaries of nationality and sovereignty coincide is one condition of such a re-establishment. Professional differentiation and the associated growth of autonomous professional and corporate traditions are further necessary conditions. The former would provide the unity and the sense of affinity so necessary to offset the centrifugal inclinations of tribes, religions, professions, and classes. The latter would provide the impetus toward pluralism so necessary to offset the centripetal inclinations of any incumbent elite. Both of these depend upon the successful extension of education throughout the society, and this can only occur if there is sufficient economic development. But an economic development great enough to permit the expansion of educational opportunity without a corresponding expansion of employment opportunity for the educated will generate restless agitation. It will swell the bureaucracy with useless hands and discontented minds and will fill cafés and crowd street corners with loungers waiting to be swept into turbulence. Under such conditions, constitutional government is unlikely either to be established where it once existed or maintained where it still exists.

In general, constitutional government in the new states seems to be in danger of being lost between the preoccupations of governments which have large aspirations and few resources and the preoccupations of governments with no aspirations except to remain in power regardless of the judgment of their citizens. In neither situation will governments be able to relax or deliberately restrict their powers.

If the governments of the second type prevail, the re-establishment or the new establishment of constitutional government seems to be a remote prospect. If governments of the first type prevail, the chances for the renewal of constitutional government in the near future are still not very good. Still, economic development is bound to produce the professions and institutions which are necessary for constitutional government, even though in the short run they might not be sufficient. Yet, it is important to remember that constitutional government in Europe arose out of a background of absolutist and tyrannical regimes and that the same might happen again in Asia and Africa.

THE POSSIBILITY OF PLURALISM:
CHURCH AND STATE IN
WEST AFRICA

James O'Connell

Ever since Christianity has come into history with its specific claim to power distinct from temporal power, the issue of church-state relations appears constantly as a confrontation, and even conflict, between the two social forms.[1] Both forms create administrative structures, often on a large scale. And both forms exact kinds of loyalty from their members that transcend other loyalties. In practice they can avoid conflict only through a careful demarcation of spiritual and temporal spheres that is more or less accepted by both sides. In cultures outside the West—as in the West itself before the advent of

1. By "state" I mean the basic political unit, that is, a grouping of men who are organized under authority in a defined territory for the pursuit of temporal common welfare, the maintenance of order, and the carrying on of external relations with other groups similarly organized. Hence a state is normally characterized by an explicitly acknowledged form of government which is able when necessary to use coercive power, by defined criteria of membership, a legal system, territorial boundaries recognized internally and externally, and diplomatic relations with other states.

The context makes clear when "church" is used to designate the totality of the Christian groups or one or the other of them. To describe what "church" means in this paper we might best turn to the *Actes de la VIe Assemblée Pleniere de l'Episcopat du Congo* (Leopoldville, 1961), p. 21: "The Church is the gathering of all the children of God in Christ. . . . She appears first as a gathering, that is, a society, an organized assembly of faithful, and an *ensemble* of means that the Lord has prepared to lead men to communion with him. Like every society the Church has its structure, its cadres, its leaders. . . . But she is not to be reduced to her outward appearance. More deeply, the Church is the Communion of men with God and of all of them with one another in Christ." "Catholic" and "Protestant" are used in this paper much as they are used in West Africa.

Christianity—there was little sense of final distinction between political and religious authority. Hence the coming of
the Christian church among West African peoples raised the
principle of the distinction of spheres and of loyalties in ways
with which African society had previously had no experience.[2]
However, there was in this respect to be a period of Western
mediation, the colonial period, during which the churches
lived with an authoritarian quasi-state that made little or no
attempt to interfere in directly spiritual matters.

The colonial period has passed and the churches now are
faced with cohabiting with the governments of newly independent states which, while they may not repudiate all colonial settlements, are by no means going to adhere slavishly
to the precedent set by them. New political circumstances
bring new problems and tensions. In discussing church-state
relations, there is considerable methodological value in focus-
ing attention on problems and tensions. As a method it serves
to throw light more easily on dynamic elements in the relations. But in making some use of this method in discussing
church-state relations in independent West African countries,
it is important not to overlook the fact that the basic patterns
of relations are coexistence, and even co-operation, rather
than conflict or tension. The same can be said of most periods
of Western history.[3]

The central issue that colors politico-religious relations in
West Africa is that the Christian churches with their deep

2. For practical purposes I am taking West Africa to be made up of the
following countries: Senegal, Mali, Guinea, Sierra Leone, Ivory Coast, Liberia,
Upper Volta, Ghana, Togo, Dahomey, Niger, Nigeria, Cameroun Republic.
One might argue that Mauritania should be included. Inevitably in a paper
of this kind the generalizations made do not apply to all the countries or to
each country in the same way. Also, the observations made have less relevance
to Liberia than to the other countries.

3. Apart from Mauritania, which declares Islam to be its state religion, the
other states either explicitly or implicitly declare themselves to be secular
states. Mali, Cameroun Republic, and Upper Volta, for example, say in their
constitutions that they are "democratic, secular and social." But in various
ways freedom in religion is constitutionally safeguarded—in Nigeria it is
written into the human rights section of the constitution.

claim on loyalties and their relatively developed organizational structures have to cohabit with new states whose governments are faced with difficult problems of national unity, economic development, and international action. To perform their tasks these governments will require great powers. In the process they may want to arrogate all powers to themselves, and so the churches may be driven to resist such tendencies and come into conflict with the state. The temptation of the state to suppress other groups, whether they be churches or trade unions, may be reinforced by the difficulty, if not the impossibility, of its own efforts to deal with national underdevelopment. Given the shortages of capital, skills, and resources that exist, the "likelihood is very great that for the majority of nations now attempting the long climb [towards economic "take-off"] the outcome in our time will be defeat."[4] The legitimacy of the new governments is apt to remain fragile, dependent as legitimacy usually is on a combination of consent (people consider that this is the right government to rule) and functionalism (people consider that the government is succeeding in its job). As well as coping with the problems of economic development, governments in some countries will have to face opposition groups that are not always ready to undertake the long work of attrition that has characterized parliamentary opposition in a country like Sweden and that are ready to toy with faster methods of vaulting into power. Altogether apart from maintaining an uneasy rule, the governments are themselves composed of men who, no matter how ill-fitted they are for ruling or how badly they do their tasks, will not stop at mere constitutional methods for insuring that they stay in power. This is the reverse side of opposition impatience. These various factors, militating against pluralism,[5] may be reinforced by a typically African

4. R. L. Heilbroner, *The Great Ascent: The Struggle for Economic Development in our Time* (New York, 1963), p. 19.

5. By "pluralism" I mean the acceptance in a society that interest groups should be able to organize effectively. In other words, not only does diversity exist in this kind of society but it is agreed among the members of the society that it has the right to exist.

unwillingness, springing from community experience under pretechnological conditions, to accept cleavages and dissent in a community. This attitude has played no small part in the forming of one-party systems in the former French territories and in the attempt to build an already huge parliamentary majority into an overwhelming one in Northern Nigeria.

These introductory considerations are simply meant to draw attention to the fact that many factors at work in the new states militate against the possibility of the continued existence of a church whose claim on human loyalty and whose organizational set-up provide both a theoretical justification and a practical framework for limiting the power of the political authorities. At the least these considerations suggest that relations will not be easy and that the ecclesiastical authorities will have to bring into play a certain suppleness in their policy, as civil rulers mobilize all the resources they can to pursue the tangible and immediately pressing tasks of social and economic development.

However, to try to understand the West African church-state situation it will be best to take a brief look at its historical evolution. That will enable us to see how matters stood as the new states came into being. Three case histories of conflict or tension will throw light on adjustment problems after independence. But an analysis of some general trends will then help to explain why the more normal pattern of church-state relations is coexistence and co-operation. Finally, it should be possible to draw some conclusions from our descriptions and analysis.

I. *Historical Background*

Christianity came initially to West Africa in a missionary wave that followed the fifteenth-century Portuguese and Spanish voyaging along the West Coast. But the resistance of the traditional religious beliefs, the failure of the new faith to cope with the indigenous social structure, the decimation of the missionaries by disease, and the absence of a sufficient number of African priests led to the wiping-out of the early endeavors (as in Warri where they had continued down to the end of the eighteenth century) or to the achievement of a merely stunted planting (as on the Island of Gorée). The present establishment of the Christian church derives from the renewed European interest in the West Coast of Africa that began to surge in the early nineteenth century and that led eventually to the setting up of British, French, and German colonies. A random sample of dates gives an idea of the pattern of the missionary arrivals: the Church Missionary Society established a solid footing in Sierra Leone in 1824 and in Western Nigeria in 1846; the Protestant Episcopal Church of America in Liberia, 1845; the Church of Scotland Mission in Calabar, 1846; the Roman Catholic Mission in Senegal, 1845; Togo, 1860; and Nigeria, 1861; the Bremen Misssion in Togo, 1847; the Basle Mission in the Gold Coast, 1824; and the Methodist Missionary Society in the Gold Coast, 1835.

Though the missionaries followed on the earlier contacts made by the traders and made use of the administrative apparatus of the colonial powers, they went earlier than the traders (who long worked through middlemen) into the hinterland away from the coast, and earlier than the colonial administrators they set up permanent stations among many coastal and hinterland peoples. The administrators sometimes accepted them as the religious arm of the "pacification" and often protected them. But at other times the administrators, especially the French who were quite ambivalent about how much anticlericalism was to be exported, hampered their work.[6] Occasionally there were bitter disputes between ad-

6. Virginia Thompson and Richard Adloff write: "Separation of Church and state in France [sic] at the turn of the century dealt a severe blow to Catholic missions throughout French West Africa, especially in Senegal, and for some years it arrested their expansion." *French West Africa* (Stanford, 1957), p. 580.

ministrators and missionaries. The British colonial authorities prevented or limited missionary activity in Muslim areas.
But by and large missionary enterprise benefited from the
colonial legal order and made use of the technology and communication system that both government and commerce developed. The missionaries also shared in the general prestige
of white colonial power that was in the process of breaking
the nerve of the traditional African cultural order and shattering the strength of much of its political rule. In other
words, the religious impact of the missionaries formed part of
and reinforced the general cultural impact of the Western
world on the African communities. The latter, overwhelmed
militarily and outpaced technologically, almost inevitably accepted that their own culture was inferior in almost all respects, and a long period was to elapse before any widespread
belief in the value of African culture would gain ground
among formally educated Africans. In some ways the missionaries more than any other group opposed aspects of the
traditional order, consecrated as the latter was by pervading
religious systems to which the missionaries were directly opposed. It was going to be a long time before Christian theolo-
gians, stimulated by the African nationalist movement, inspired by their own biblical revival, and informed by anthropological research, would recognize the positive worth of the
metaphysical insights in African religion and assert that
Christianity had to build on them rather than destroy them.[7]

It is worthwhile to describe briefly the stages of growth of

7. Eventually, however, many Christian missionaries were ahead of most
educated Africans in promoting the revival of African culture. What Chief
Awolowo says of one of them who taught at Wesley College, Ibadan, is worth
quoting: "The Principal of the College in my time, the Rev. E. H. Nightingale, B. D., suffered a good deal of unjustified criticism. Essentially his view
was that we should be proud of anything that was indigenous to us; our
language, our culture and our style of dress. . . . It was believed that Mr.
Nightingale fostered these policies in order to slow down our progress in the
Western sense. I shared this view then, but I now think that he was a great
pioneer. Practically all his critics are today doing precisely what he preached
many years ago." *Awo: The Autobiography of Chief Abafemi Awolowo*
(London, 1960), p. 64.

the colonial quasi-state and its merging into an independent African state and to notice a somewhat parallel growth of an ecclesiastical order.[8] (*1*) *Pioneering stage*: This stage includes the exploits of some of the explorers, the military leaders who made the first treaties (Lugard, for example) and early administrators (Sir Harry Johnston). It establishes an important set of roles, heroic in their proportions, and a mythology of uplift which becomes the first legitimizing basis for colonial rule. (*2*) *Politico-administrative stage*: A settled though rudimentary administration is built up in this period. The field officer who constantly tours and who links his administration with the administration of the traditional chiefs (over which he wields a veto) is the key figure. (*3*) *Bureaucratic-colonial stage*: This period develops in large part out of the need for specialization of function and division of labor that is imposed by the more ambitious tasks which social welfare colonialism sets for itself. Administration grows more stable as well as more highly organized. Expatriate civil servants and the growing number of expatriates employed by the large commercial firms live in communities of their own, much further removed from Africans than had been their predecessors. In this period the theory that justifies colonial rule shifts from a lofty moral basis to one based on efficiency and skilled manpower. The beginnings of a developed African school system appear. And African nationalism and a desire for self-government begin to grow. (*4*) *Self-government and independence*: The colonial governments acknowledge that a sufficiently large group of educated Africans is at hand to govern. Rather than face continual agitation and possible disturbances, they hand over power to Africans through various stages of self-government into complete independence. The colonial bureaucracy (gradually however being Afri-

8. The stages of colonialism and introduction of representative government outlined in the text are taken from David E. Apter, *The Political Kingdom in Uganda* (Princeton, N. J., 1961), pp. 447-459. I have, however, modified Professor Apter's stages slightly.

canized) manages the administration and public institutions such as the statutory corporations during this period. But with independence (in southern Nigeria before independence) the Africanization of the bureaucracy is hastened. And the political decisions are now completely in the hands of African leaders who nonetheless have to reckon with states whose unity is fragile, whose economies are underdeveloped, and whose freedom of action in the international scene is to some extent hampered by continued economic links (especially in the case of the former French territories) with the former colonial powers.

The equivalent stages of ecclesiastical growth are: (*1*) *Pioneering stage*: A man like Father Borghero (Dahomey and Nigeria) and his immediate successors work as an advance party. They show that people are receptive to evangelization and that disease is not the impossible obstacle to expatriate missionaries that it was once thought to be. The missionaries of this period establish stations on the coast or near the coast. But they make journeys into the interior that affect the future pattern of mission development. (*2*) *Head mission stage*: From a few central missions missionaries go on tour and call on different areas several times a year. Shortage of personnel prevents the setting-up of permanent residences in the out-stations. In between missionary visits a catechist serves a little group of Christians. Almost from the start each central station possesses a school, and some out-stations do. (*3*) *Diocesan and parish erection stage*: More priests become available; in part the stream of expatriate missionaries increases, in part numbers of African priests are being ordained. In the Catholic mission set-up, mission stations give way to parishes, and parishes are grouped under dioceses that succeed the old vicariates and prefectures. Other denominations similarly enlarge the organization of their work and turn out (the Anglicans better than the Catholics by far) numbers of African priests. At the same time the medical and social work of the missions has grown considerably. And the governments, especially in the British territories, are willing to work through the mission structure to expand primary and secondary school systems. (*4*) *National ecclesiastical stage*: Most of the Protestant bodies have become independent. In countries like Nigeria, Anglicans, Methodists, and Presbyterians pursue serious unity talks, aware in an African context that many, if not all, the issues that divide them are historical and social rather than doctrinal. The Catholic dioceses organize nationally in a new way. Though many bishops are still foreigners, it is recognized that it is only a matter of time before Africans take over the leadership posts. Catholic expansion however is a long way ahead of the number of available African priests and an end to the need for foreign missionaries is not yet in sight.

From this brief historical sketch of colonial and missionary development we want to select two themes for some further slight expansion: (*a*) growth of education and (*b*) ecclesiastical reaction to nationalism.

a. Schools sponsored by official representatives of the colonizing powers—as well as schools sponsored by private agencies such as missionary bodies and groups of merchants—were as old on the west coast as the quasi-permanent European settlements. But before long the initiative in this kind of formal education went over to the missionaries who alone had the organization and the motivation to bear the brunt of the work in the early period. The civil authorities helped in many instances. But it was not until into the third stage (bureaucratic-colonial) that the governments gave substantial aid to private schools. In their schools the missionaries were spurred by a number of motives: they wanted their converts to be able to read the Bible and to become familiar with new religious and socio-moral notions; they discovered that the people who rejected their teaching were willing to risk having their children indoctrinated in return for an instruction in reading, writing, and arithmetic; they used the long period of schooling to give a character formation to young people; and, not least, they saw that those they trained were able to better their condition in the world. The last point is important. The mission schools prospered because they fulfilled a real economic function. As administration and commerce expanded, there was need for indigenous auxiliaries who filled the lower posts and were much less expensive than expatriates. The education given was literary. Often the schools were criticized for that; early colonial reports foreshadow later reports under self-government that lament the absence of technical education. But the missionaries had neither the capital nor the skills required for technical education. And in any case, a politico-legal administration (which even now is only slowly changing) and a trading economy held out principally a demand for clerks. In this demand also lay the source of the reproaches addressed to the missions for turning out uprooted, half-educated generations of Africans who moved awkwardly in both a tribal world and a Western world. But it was these products of the mission schools who were, for the most part, to lay the foundations for a new African self-awareness, and eventual national consciousness.

The upshot of the mission concern with education was that as the various territories approached self-government the mission bodies—though they were subject to government control and inspection in their schoolwork—had in their hands an enormous part of the administration of education.[9] This situation meant that a large amount of ecclesiastical energy

9. A rough outline of elementary school figures gives an indication of the importance of the missions in education. In Senegal the Catholic mission operates 281 classrooms out of the country's total 2,233 classrooms; in Mali mission bodies operate 42 schools out of 425; in Sierra Leone mission bodies operate 468 out of 523 schools; in the Ivory Coast mission bodies operate 500 of the 1,551 schools; in the Upper Volta 41 per cent of the schools are mission schools; in Ghana mission bodies operate 3,201 out of 4,546 schools; in Togo mission schools taught 42,112 of the 87,461 children in elementary schools; about 50 per cent of the children at school in Dahomey are in mission schools; 7.3 per cent of children in Niger are in mission schools; over 70 per cent of the children at school in Nigeria are in mission schools; in the Cameroun Republic 2,013 of the 2,471 schools are mission schools. These figures are for the most part 1959 figures. I have taken them from Helen Kitchen, ed., *The Educated African* (New York, 1962).

154 DEVELOPMENT: FOR WHAT?

went into quite secular aspects of school organization. It meant also that a situation existed that for several reasons the new political leaders would inevitably question: (1) Education plays a central role in the creation of a national spirit and identity. Political leaders are usually unhappy to leave this task in private rather than public hands. Also in countries where great stress is being placed on unity, the denominational control of education tends to be regarded as divisive. (2) The religious ideology of the churches has been imported; their work has gone on for a long time in collaboration with the colonial regime, following curricula that were often enough little adapted to African history or values; and actual control of the schools in many cases remained under the supervision of foreign priests. In short, political leaders sometimes made the charge themselves, and they were sensitive to the charge when made by others: that education could not be truly national while it was in the hands of the churches. But against these considerations was the fact that the missions were willing to move with the times and the government could exercise final control over curricula and examinations. And governments that were beginning to discover how costly administration was were thinking twice before adding substantially to administrative work by substituting themselves for the religious bodies in educational administration.[10]

b. The period that lasted from the end of World War II to 1958 was the critical time in which the African nationalist movements took decisive shape and spelled out their objectives. By 1950 it had become clear that independence for most of the countries was little more than a few years away. At the end of the war the Christian religious bodies were still for the most part controlled by expatriates. They were ini-

10. A Sierra Leone white paper on education observes, for example, that the government ". . . fully appreciates that more than half the existing primary school accommodation in Freetown is already provided by the Churches . . . [who] provide for 20 classrooms to absorb some 600 children." *White Paper on Educational Development* (Freetown, 1958), p. 4.

tially bewildered and frightened by the emergence of African nationalism and—to say the least—did not take kindly to it. Many of them were convinced that Africans were not ready to govern themselves. Moreover they had worked out a modus vivendi with the colonial authorities, men of their own culture whose reactions were largely predictable, and they saw little but insecurity in political change.[11] These fears were not eased and the churchmen were not rendered more kindly disposed towards the nationalist movement when some nationalists in their new-found sense of things African began to attack Christianity as a foreign importation; other nationalists went even further to castigate missionaries bitterly and unfairly as imperialist minions whose main function had been to reconcile Africans to the colonial conquest. What further upset religious leaders in the French territories was the link of Felix Houphouêt-Boigny and the *Rassemblement Démocratique Africaine* with the French Communist Party that lasted until 1950. And formed as they were in the older European tradition where socialism and anticlericalism went hand-in-hand, the missionaries were little equipped to understand African socialist aspirations and emphases.

Only belatedly did most churchmen recognize the inevitable victory of the independence movement, begin to glimpse its positive values, and set out to work within its context. To some extent, however, many churchmen have not recovered from the insecurity of this period. One writer, commenting on the Catholic church in the new French-speaking states, says: "In the face of political regimes which at worst have been hostile and at best complacent, the Church has reacted with indecision, uncertainty, and, at times, excessive caution."[12] Undoubtedly the church lost some good will among African nationalists by its initial failure to appreciate and

11. Adloff and Thompson point out: "Since World War II the attitude of the French Government towards both Catholic and Protestant missions in the Federation has mellowed." *Op. cit.*, p. 582.

12. Victor D. DuBois, "Recent Trends in French-Speaking West Africa," *Africa Report* (March, 1963), p. 15.

sympathize with the independence movement. However, many Christian nationalists were able to distinguish between their religious allegiance and their political aspirations. They also recognized that missionaries, even those opposed to nationalism, had served the countries devotedly and had been foremost in organizing the schools that lay behind the development of nationalism. Finally, some left-wing priests helped the nationalist leaders in many ways, and papers like *Afrique Nouvelle* and the *Nigerian Catholic Herald* gave articulate and outspoken support to the maturer nationalist claims.[13]

II. *Three Case Histories of Conflict and Tension*

It is against the background of the history that has been sketched, the problems that the new states have to face, the spiritual objectives that the churches pursue, and the temporal involvements that they are committed to that we can turn to consider three case histories of conflict or tension that have marked the progress of contemporary West African church-state relations.

1. *Guinea and private schools*

In January, 1959, President Sékou Touré announced that Guinea was setting up a national plan for education and that, in the course of its implementation, private schools (mainly Catholic with a few Protestant) would be taken over; in the meantime, however, they would receive subsidies as usual. This policy was in keeping with the general Guinean attempt

---

13. On the contribution made by Christian missionary influences to the African nationalist movement James S. Coleman has several interesting observations. He points out, for example, the influence exerted by groups in the United Kingdom and the United States: ". . . the host function of Christian groups and individual Christian spokesmen in the two countries has been a significant element in the development of Nigerian nationalism. More conservative or more cautious Christians might have considered such activity as premature or improper, or even left-wing; nevertheless, it is a strand in the Christian-missionary influence which has been under-estimated, particularly by the nationalists themselves." *Nigeria: Background to Nationalism* (Berkeley and Los Angeles, 1958), p. 111.

to plan its economy and its manpower skills on a national level, to organize all groups through the party, and to create a national identity through unity of effort and doctrine. Speaking against teachers who disagreed with "teaching politics" in the schools, Sékou Touré insisted: "For them [the teachers] the young must know nothing about politics. As if the facts of politics were not the condensation of economic, social, and cultural facts!"[14] Similarly in creating a single national youth organization, Sékou Touré said: "a goodly number of our comrades believe that liberty consists in letting everyone do and say what he pleases, in letting every class of youth organize as it wishes and take what initiative it pleases. Well, the Party . . . does not agree. For the Party . . . liberty is only a tool, a tool for organizing and orienting our activities to conform with the popular will."[15] Other statements went even further in a totalitarian direction.

Catholics in Guinea form a tiny minority—25,000 from a population of 2,500,000. Uneasy as they were about the direction of policy and the relations being opened up with Communist-bloc countries, the Catholic leaders hesitated to take a stand. But the schools were nationalized sooner than was expected in mid-1961 and at the same time Sékou Touré indicated scathingly that his government wanted no non-Guineans in charge of religious bodies in their country. The Archbishop de Milleville of Conakry was provoked by the nationalization and by Touré's comments to send the president a letter in which he made a traditional and moderate exposition of the relations between church and state. The Guinean government reacted by immediately expelling the Archbishop. Sékou Touré declared that in the future "no Catholic prelate except an African would be accredited to Guinea." After the expulsion the Apostolic Delegate, resid-

14. *Action Politique du Parti Démocratique de Guinée pour l'Emancipation Africaine* (Conakry, 1959), p. 413.
15. *La Liberté* (April 10, 1959), p. 4.

ing at Dakar, went to Guinea to hold consultations with the government. Not long afterwards a Guinean was appointed Archbishop of Conakry, and the government sent representatives to the consecration ceremony.

This particular crisis became acute because it involved issues that seemed vital to both sides. The stand of the church challenged the claim of a one-party authoritarian state to mobilize all groups in a monolithic way and to politicize the entire social life of the country. The failure of the church to Africanize its leadership and personnel also exacerbated Guinean feelings that were still raw both from the traumatic step of saying "no" to De Gaulle and from the abrupt and wantonly destructive withdrawal of French personnel at the moment of independence. The move of the state to take over the schools, no matter what warning had been given, threatened a sphere in which the modern church has consistently battled for rights and a sphere which in West Africa has also been a leading means of conversion and instruction. The insistence on Guinean leadership in the church upset an existing situation of French missionary leadership. But more important, it threatened the principle of the right of the church to name its own leaders. In the upshot the Guinean state was seen to be rather less totalitarian than some statements might have suggested. And the church recognized that useful though the schools were the Christian apostolate was not irremediably tied to them.

That the Guinean authorities did not feel obliged to oust the church from the country is an indication that their declared aim to politicize the organizational structures of the country is in practice limited to exercising control over forces that are decisive in creating a national image and national unity, in deciding the legitimacy of government, and in contributing to manpower formation and economic growth. The organizational confines of the party structure and the relatively little developed civil service cadres make impossible the kind of totalitarian control that the complex and pervasive Russian bureaucracy achieved. At one stage the kind of organization that had been achieved in Guinea gave the impression that Sékou Touré and the *Parti Démocratique de Guinée* would carry Guinea faster towards modernization than any similar African country.[16] But now a lot of the effort and idealism has faltered.[17] It is clear that too much organization was attempted too soon and that it was not possible to plan the economy as thoroughly as the party leadership desired.[18] It is also clear that the Guinean people were not ready to accept the rigidly conceived communal labor designated as *investissements humains*. The Guinean leaders, in fact, overestimated their own capacities and underestimated the problems that would arise in the course of socioeconomic reform. The consequence has been political discontent manifested in the teachers' strike in 1961 and peasant disturbances in 1960 and 1961. However, the Guinean government has shown considerable suppleness in its capacities to revise its policies. And it has shown a seriousness and thoughtfulness of purpose that governments in other developing areas have not often matched.

It is difficult to sympathize with the Catholic authorities for the long years of lack of foresight that left the church with so few Guinean priests and so little Guinean leader-

16. The Guinean effort to expand education has some striking successes: "In 1958, on the eve of independence, there were 1,500 pupils in Guinea qualified to receive the CEP (Elementary School Certificate). By 1959, this number had increased to 4,000. In comparison to 900 students admitted to the first form in 1958, the following year saw the same group augmented by nearly 100 per cent to 1,750. In 1959, primary schools, both public and private, had a total enrollment of 52,000 pupils. By April, 1960, this figure had climbed to 84,000." Victor D. DuBois in Kitchen, *The Educated African,* p. 537.

17. René Dumont of whose devotion to African causes there can be little doubt describes the "Guinean adventure" in his *L'Afrique noire est mal partie* (Paris, 1962). He remarks simply: "The Guineans were not willing to make the necessary efforts and accept the discipline needed for the measures they adopted. . . ." p. 227.

18. A correspondent in *West Africa*, July 21, 1961, in an article, "Education in Guinea," wrote: "The lack of able administrative staff to put these decisions into effect [decisions dealing with the organization of education] has resulted in inefficiency and no little confusion."

ship at the moment of independence. However, the refusal
to accept the contribution of the French Catholic priests in
organizing education foreshadowed the resentment that the
Russian technologists would meet as they urged governmental efficiency on the Guineans. Earlier the French trading
firms had been expropriated and a United Nations technical
assistance team was obliged to leave the country when its efforts had been spurned. For this somewhat doctrinaire ill-will
towards foreigners, Guinea has paid a heavy price in a slower
than necessary pace of economic growth and in the trading
failures of the *Comptoirs Guinéens de Commerce Extérieur.*
Foreign aid may need to be looked at carefully and trading
firms certainly should be controlled. But Guinea—or any
West African country—cannot afford to reject easily foreign
skills or not to make use of the good will that exists in many
parts of the developed world toward the efforts of the new
states.

2. *Ghana and socialist flexibility*[19]

Addressing the Anglican Synod of Accra in August, 1962,
the bishop of Accra, the Right Reverend R. R. Roseveare,
denounced the godlessness of the instruction being handed
out to members of the Young Pioneer Movement and the
extravagant cult of President Nkrumah's personality within
the movement. The Bishop said: "Not only myself, but all
Heads of Churches in Ghana, are shocked by the Godlessness of this Movement and by some of its phrases and songs
prescribed for the children to repeat or sing. We made our
views known to the Minister of Education last April, saying that we found it impossible to give our support and
co-operation in the development of the Movement as at present constituted. Moreover, it seems that the Movement con-
fuses the work and example of a great man with Divine Acts

19. In writing this section I have been able to draw on Professor David E.
Apter's "The Politics of Solidarity in Ghana" which is to appear in James S.
Coleman and Carl G. Rosberg, *Political Parties of Tropical Africa.*

which are unique in history. This incipient atheism is quite foreign to the traditional concept of the African personality." The movement was founded in part to absorb some unemployed school-leavers and to make use of them in socially valuable labor fields and in part to have at hand an élite band of young people, highly indoctrinated in Nkrumaism and dedicated politically, who could be used to spearhead the organizing of young people generally in Ghana. Carrying on the African praise-song tradition, the Young Pioneers indulged in the most extravagant lauding of the President and heaped on him attributes that in some cases derived from Christian worship and were meant to convey the divine omnipotence.[20] Just at this time extreme socialist tendencies also seemed to be gaining ground among the leaders of the Convention People's Party grouped around the president. Some Christian clerics believed that Ghana was being guided toward a form of totalitarianism, if not toward a completely Communist state, as leaders issued threats to nationalize all private enterprise and as government-sponsored organizations such as the National Council of Ghana Women, the Co-operative Movement, and the Trade Union Council set up links with international Communist bodies. By and large the churches had not reacted strongly in the face of what was going on. More than one cleric, however, had criticized the ruling party's ideological outpourings, and nothing happened except that individual clerics were criticized by party leaders or party newspapers. The churches generally were hampered by distrust of their own capacity to face the power of the state. In

20. The following paragraph—from the *Evening News*—is an example of the kind of material that was upsetting the Christians: "Nkrumah is our Messiah. Whoever sees his brother's need and supplies it—not by casting off the discarded garment to him—but by giving him a moral and spiritual standard by which he shall live; that is the Messiah, the Saviour, the Christ. ... Long before Jesus, were men like Moses, Joshua, Elisha, etc. who demonstrated the true idea of sonship. This demonstration is by no means ended with Jesus. Why! Karl Marx demonstrated the Christ, and so did Lenin of U.S.S.R., Gandhi of India, Moa [*sic*] of China and in our midst is Kwame Nkrumah." Cited in Apter, "The Politics of Solidarity in Ghana" *loc. cit.*

any case they were also unsure of how they might best interpret events and did not know if they had sufficient reason to
enter into direct conflict with the government.

Bishop Roseveare chose a very sensitive moment to speak.
A bomb had just been thrown at the president. The publicity
given to his criticisms jostled in the newspapers with the aftermath of the bomb explosion. The party organs, *Ghanaian
Times* and *Evening News,* turned on him with bitter vicious-
ness, even suggested that he was a foreigner who had been in
some way associated with the bomb plotting, and demanded
that he be expelled. He was called to the office of the Minister
of the Interior, Mr. Kwaku Boateng, who told him: "It is the
opinion of the Government that the Church must never interfere with any Government policies." His residence permit
was withdrawn, and he was expelled. Archbishop Patterson
of the West African Province, who was visiting Ghana at the
time and who publicly supported Bishop Roseveare against
the attacks being made on him, was also required to leave
the country.

Two interesting reactions followed in Christian opinion.
The first was that, unlike the Catholic bending before the
breeze in Guinea, the Ghanaian Anglicans resisted vocally.
The Anglican Synod of Accra stood firm behind its bishop.
The second was that the reaction to the incident spread be-
yond the Ghanaian frontier, especially to Nigeria where
people were also incensed at the expulsion of Archbishop
Patterson. The Governor of Eastern Nigeria, Sir Francis
Ibiam, sent a telegram to a Synod of West African Anglican
bishops being held at Lagos: "I strongly support Bishop
Roseveare for denouncing Godlessness of Ghana Young Pioneers." The eastern government-owned newspaper, *Nigerian
Outlook,* said that the Bishop would not have been doing his
duty if he had shut his eyes to what he had condemned. However, the Bishop owed at least part of his support from the
government-owned newspaper to the ill-feeling that existed

at the time between the Ghana and Nigerian governments.

At much the same time as Christian opinion reacted vigorously, two ministers—Tawia Adamafio, Minister of Information and Broadcasting and Ako Adjei, Minister of Foreign
Affairs—and several party leaders were put under preventive
detention. They were suspected of having been implicated in
bomb attacks. These men were also part of the kernel of the
group that had been pushing extreme socialist views and that
had been using adulation of the president as a means of getting their views across. Though sticking to socialist views the
president brought back old guard leaders, Kofi Baako and
Kojo Botsio, who had been eliminated previously in the name
of socialist purity, and Nathaniel Welbeck, who had been out
of favor for having messed up assignments in Guinea and the
Congo. What these men had in common was tried loyalty to
Nkrumah and a future which was linked to his. This was in
contrast to the attitude of the imprisoned leaders who had
clearly looked on the president as dispensable. Nkrumah himself was dismayed by some of the socially disruptive effects
of a socialism that had got out of hand and was shaken by
plots that appeared to come from associates who had most fostered fulsome adulation of him.

Apart from the timing of his address, which was decidedly
unfortunate, Bishop Roseveare had largely been the victim of
party groups led or heavily influenced by this apparently
Marxist (it is difficult to say how sincere the Marxism was),
anti-religious, and xenophobiac faction. The latter used the
name and influence of the president to legitimize their doctrinal orientation and to turn the bishop into a scapegoat for
opposition to the president. Bishop Roseveare himself insisted
that his expulsion could not have been known beforehand to
the president—and it is true that for some time decisions on
quite important matters had been taking place without the
president's knowledge. Bishop Roseveare also insisted that he
saw no incompatibility between belief in God and socialism

and that he himself had been "politically a socialist for years." These were wise insistencies in a country where policy had little choice except to be socialist and where power was very much personalized. Nkrumah's approach to socialism had never been doctrinaire, and he had never shown himself either antireligious or anti-Christian. He was simply deeply convinced that the state had to take the initiative constantly and provide both capital and organizational strength in the conditions of African underdevelopment.

In recent times, since the fall of those whom Professor Apter calls the "socialist opportunists," there has been a new stress on the role of the civil service and the party has been reorganized in the constituencies. The Christian churches are not looked on as offering doctrinal opposition to a presidential leadership in which Nkrumah increasingly looks like a modernized version of a traditional Ghanaian chief. Rather are their efforts welcome as part of the social and economic effort of the nation. Expelled in August, 1961, Bishop Roseveare was allowed to return in November of the same year. The return of the bishop underlines the pragmatic approach of President Nkrumah and his capacity to conciliate important sections of opinion in his own country and outside, even if this means revising a governmental decision. The attempt has been given up to "blend party, state, and society in a single community." The CPP now believes simply that loyalty should be shown to the president and political differences should be worked out within the party fold. Other social differences, including religious ones, are not expected to be rejected and are being treated with a new respect.

3. *Eastern Nigeria and religious politics*

Addressing a group of Catholic students at the University of Nigeria Nsukka, in May, 1961, the Archbishop of Onitsha, Dr. Charles Heerey, made comments in which he warned Nigerians against having anything to do with communism.

The remarks were banal enough and the kind that might have been expected. But as soon as they were reported in the press, there was uproar. From many sides condemnations of the archbishop's stand poured in. Two explicit charges were made against him in newspaper columns, in letters to the editor, and in speeches made by politicians. One was that he was a churchman interfering in politics. The other was that he was a foreigner trying to impose foreign views on Nigeria. In other words many Nigerians were contending that their leaders could make their own way ahead without clerical strictures or foreign advice. But behind the explicit charges lay a situation in the eastern region of Nigeria in which religious cleavages, political competition, and anticlerical resentment over schools ignited other issues.

In Eastern Nigeria, Roman Catholics and Anglicans are fairly evenly matched in numbers, though in recent years the Catholics have expanded more rapidly. Strong rivalry might be expected in these circumstances, and in fact it does exist. Other factors aggravate the rivalry: Nigerian Anglicanism derives from a Low Church outlook that is traditionally hostile to the Church of Rome; and Nigerian Catholicism has been built up by Irish priests who cherish a nationalist as well as a religious dislike of Anglicanism. These several factors have sharpened the edge of religious competition and have led in some instances to bitter and undignified scrambles among communities to found, or to take over, schools and hospitals. When elections began to be held in the region, religious differences made their way over into the political field. In the largely one-party Ibo country, what counted was to secure the NCNC (National Council of Nigeria and the Cameroons) nomination. Candidates mustered all the influence they could, and that sometimes included religious support. In some areas, undoubtedly, ministers of different denominations urged privately or publicly that a nomination should go to the candidate who was a member of their denomination. Two predominantly lay organizations—one Anglican, the other Catholic[21]—were widely suspected of lobbying for candidates, and even of providing funds to facilitate the securing of nominations by certain candidates. Given this situation, it is obvious why "religious politics" came to be used as a term to designate an undesirable form of political conflict. But we must be careful not to oversimplify. In most eastern constituencies the issue of "religious politics" did not arise. In certain cases where it did arise, it arose not because candidates were representatives of religious blocs but because one or more candidates set out to raise all the support possible and make capital out of a religious affiliation. In other cases the religious issue was built into generation-long rivalry in areas where towns or lineages had adopted different forms of Christianity and old rivalries surfaced in the guise of religious politics. But the marginal cases of conflict obtained a publicity out of proportion to their importance. They also evoked bitterness out of proportion. And they helped to confirm Catholics and Protestants generally in religious distrust of one another.

The sharp reaction to the archbishop's comments occurred when the battle for nominations in the regional elections was about to become intense. Those responsible for the public attacks were mainly eastern (and indeed Ibo) non-Catholic political activists. What was surprising was the initial slowness of the Catholics to come to the defense of the archbishop. This may be explained by two reasons: (1) Many Nigerians, belonging to all denominations in the south, resent clerics making political statements. This resentment stems in part from a view, common even among Catholics, that religion has no concern with political decisions. (2) The resentment is heightened by the overwhelmingly foreign (Irish) make-up of the Catholic clergy. So uneasiness about

21. Eastern Nigeria Catholic Council and the Convention of Protestant Citizens.

the church's role in politics and embarrassment about the ethnic composition of their clergy hampered Catholics' reactions to attacks that they undoubtedly resented. But the political basis to the bitterness of the attacks was reinforced by the manner in which Nigerian Protestants seized on the opportunity to strike a blow against Catholicism as a religious organization. One Anglican priest-journalist even suggested that Nigeria might adopt an Indian solution and prohibit the entry of missionaries who were to be engaged only in pastoral work and did not justify being admitted on educational or medical welfare grounds.

Controversies wax warm easily in Nigeria, and acrimony tends to outpace the reality of the cleavages. But as the attacks on Archbishop Heerey continued longer than the few days or a week that might have been expected, the Catholics began to react. They were conscious that he was one of their religious leaders and that he had given long years of service to the country, playing especially a foremost role in organizing education. They denied that his words lent themselves to the construction put on them and asserted that what he had said was correct. Catholic critics also pointed out that in many ways it was they who had had to fight to defend themselves and to claim their rights in politics because the older intelligentsia who had long controlled things was predominantly Protestant. Catholics were particularly incensed that the government-owned *Nigerian Outlook* was, they considered, being used to launch attacks on the Catholic church. The controversy died down after some weeks. But sporadic shots continued to be fired by members of both sides. Fortunately by this time sensible Anglicans and Catholics saw that both denominations were being harmed by this internecine strife. The politicians also wanted badly to try and end "religious politics" and so eliminate at least one exacerbating factor in struggles for nominations. Talks went on behind the scenes. Finally Dr. Okpara, the premier of the region and a Methodist, several Catholic and Protestant political leaders, and religious leaders from various bodies met and agreed on co-operation among all groups to end these struggles. The agreement was given wide publicity.

Behind the outburst against Archbishop Heerey and the Catholic clergy lay an even deeper issue, especially in the long run, than what we have so far been mentioning: control of educational organization. More even than in the play of party politics, political leaders had grown to resent the role of the church in education and to regard it as an anachronism that reflected badly on the country's administrative maturity.[22] Once more—as in Guinea—the fact that many managers of primary schools and principals of secondary schools were expatriates, especially in the Catholic church, aroused fears, both genuine and hypocritical, that colonial influences would still go on existing. A final cause for concern lay in the way that denominational education split communities. The Dike Committee made observations that illustrate these points:[23]

In spite of the fact that the Voluntary Agency schools are for the most part maintained by Government funds, yet their proprietors and managers, divided as they are by rival denominations and divergent educational and economic aims, still retain firm control of these institutions. . . . Evidence abounds to show that Protestants will co-operate with Government if taken into confidence in working out a system of state education. . . . It is the view of the Committee . . . that the Catholic mission which owns and controls a little less than 50 per cent of the schools in the Region and which received well over 1 million last year from the state to run these schools, is opposed to state education. . . . Another aspect of the Catholic position to which our attention

22. The only other country where there is an antagonism to the church in education that is comparable to that in Eastern Nigeria is the Ivory Coast. There it comes in part from a strongly lay tradition in the teaching profession that derives from the French tradition; in part also—as in Eastern Nigeria—it comes from anticlerical feelings that are caused by administrative friction between the clerics who operate the mission school system and the teachers who work for them. Clerics have constantly underestimated the political hostility that has accrued to them from the latter factor.

23. *Report on the Review of the Educational System in Eastern Nigeria* (Enugu, 1962).

has been called is the clerical control of their schools. This situation, their own supporters allege, leaves little room for the advancement or promotion of laymen in their organisation. Since
Nigerian clerics have not been turned out in great numbers to
take over from foreign priests, the Nigerianisation of education,
which has taken place in the Protestant agencies, has not been
matched by a similar movement in the Catholic mission. Nevertheless even those who criticise aspects of the existing organisation
of Catholic education are not blind to its great achievement.

When the government of the eastern region decided to
introduce universal and free primary education into the region—beginning in December, 1956—it also decided that
the huge expansion of schools that the scheme would involve
should take place through the local councils. This was a clear
declaration that the state was opting in principle for a system
of public education run by secular authorities. The scheme
failed disastrously, and its failure brought a lot of odium on
the government. Primarily it failed because its financing had
not been worked out properly beforehand and it cost much
more than had been anticipated. But contributing factors in
the failure were the inefficiency and corruption of the local
councils which were responsible for the management of these
new schools, the poor quality of the teachers employed, and sub-
standard buildings and equipment. Not the least factor in the
failure however was the hostility of the Voluntary Agencies,
especially the Catholic mission, who were not prepared at
that stage to see the organizational control of the schools (the
state simply sent its inspectors and officers to control standards
and the spending of grants) pass out of their hands. Enjoying
more of the confidence of the people than the government
realized, their opposition, coupled with the low standards of
the new schools and the introduction of fees in all schools a
year after the start of the scheme, helped to trigger discontent
that broke out into rioting in certain parts of the region.
Eastern politicians with secularist leanings have not forgotten
the ill-will that the missions bore them at this period. Their

rancor against the Catholic mission was not the least reason for the attacks on this mission by the government paper.

After 1957 the numbers of children going to school dropped with the reintroduction of fees. The schools closed in consequence of the drop were mainly local council schools. Since then, where educational expansion has taken place in both primary and secondary schools, the government has tended to favor expansion through local bodies rather than through the Voluntary Agencies. But this tendency has not been firm and the members of the regional cabinet have been far from agreed on it as a policy. In fact, the government and the Agencies are continuing at present the previously existing relationship in education rather than working out a new one. It is significant that the *Report* of the Dike Committee, suggesting some changes, which was presented to the government in 1959, was not published until 1962 because the government had little desire to alienate the Catholics whose susceptibilities were offended by parts of the *Report*. The problem that the then Director of Education for Nigeria, Mr. R. A. McL. Davidson, posed in 1947 still remains: "It thus becomes essential to redefine the relationship between Government and Voluntary Agencies, so that in future, Government, Voluntary Agencies and their respective staffs know clearly their several and related responsibilities." Good will on both sides could work out a relationship that gives the state the increased role that it must eventually play, relieves the missions of organizational tasks that are diverting energy from pastoral tasks and yet gives religion its place in education. But it is doubtful if at present the state can increase its financial commitments or stretch its administrative structure much further in education without damaging its efforts in other spheres. And the churches are unlikely to want to change an existing relationship that for all the administrative burdens it imposes meets their religious requirements.

To sum up: the controversy over Archbishop Heerey's

statement, seen against the play of politics and the organization of education, throws fascinating light on the complex elements that go into the making of democracy in East Nigeria. Specifically it emphasizes: (*1*) The bid for nomination as a party candidate is so far from being completely controlled by the NCNC National Executive that candidates seek constantly to muster all the support they can in the constituencies. (*2*) The time has not yet come—though if the region should make a deliberate decision in this direction, it could come quite soon—when the state can administer the educational system as much as it does in a country like England. But many Nigerian political leaders in the east—and elsewhere—look forward to so doing. (*3*) Meantime in spite of misgivings about using religious and foreign skills the government is content to go on using them. (*4*) The Catholic church in this controversy and at other times has received due notice that her chief prelates and leading spokesmen must be Nigerians; otherwise Nigerian sensibilities are likely to continue to be affronted, and the church can hope to make little impact on public life. (*5*) The deep loyalty of the Catholic members suggests that the present price a government would pay for entering into direct conflict with the church would be much too great for it to be contemplated politically.

III. *Co-operation Rather than Conflict*

What these case histories enable us to do is to observe where latent possibilities of stress have erupted into open conflict in the postindependence period. There is hardly any West African country in which some of the trends and tensions manifest in Guinea, Ghana, and Eastern Nigeria are not to be found. Yet, though it has been important to single out these specific instances of troubled relations, it would be no better to judge the general situation from cases of conflict than it would be to construct a view of human nature from a psychiatrist's pages. Hence, it is important now to look at the general situation which by and large reflects church-state amity and cooperation and to understand the reasons that lie behind it. What we shall find is that the complaint against the foreign origin of the Christian church and the charge that Christian priests destroyed or neglected African values and traditions is no longer so freely made and that the religious and temporal contribution of the church is more deeply appreciated and more accepted than at any time since the beginning of the nationalist movement. Several reasons explain this improvement: a new emphasis and content in nationalism, social change seen as modernization rather than as Westernization, and the number and devotion of Christians.

1. *A new nationalism*

a. Though a sensitivity still remains, the inferiority complex and the hurt both taken and given in the colonial era have begun to disappear. African leaders now wield political power, and African administrators fill the top-ranking civil service posts in most of the West African countries. These men realize that they are in control of their countries, and they believe that they can handle outside contributions, no matter where these contributions come from. If the West African leaders intend to scrutinize carefully what is foreign, they intend to reject nothing simply because it is foreign. Christianity is more likely now to be asked what it is than where it came from.

b. The days of the nationalist frills when energies had to be predominantly geared to achieving political freedom have gone. Freedom is now seen to be illusory without a rising standard of living; it is seen to be fragile without a basic and minimum unity existing between the various ethnic groups that make up each country. In other words, governments are seeking to concentrate their efforts on economic growth, social welfare, and national integration. Statesmen and administrators are gladly accepting contributions that further these objectives. The Ivory Coast, Ghana, and Sierra Leone seek foreign investors and offer them safeguards; Senegal called on Père Lebret, a French Dominican priest, and a team of collaborators to work out the most concretely socialist economic plan in West Africa; Nigeria is making ample use of foreign technicians; and even Guinea and Mali have been seeking better relations with France. In the sphere of economics and social welfare, the Christian churches have helped especially in education and medicine. A great part of the educational development of most of the countries would not have taken place in the past—and could not be maintained on the same scale in the present—without the relatively inexpensive and skilled manpower and the organizational structure that the churches provide. Even the once easily made sneer that the missions did no more than turn out clerks is not easily made now. For one thing, no better system of education has so far been constructed in West Africa; for another, people are conscious that literacy, inadequate though it may be alone, is nonetheless a basic element in agriculture extension work, preventive medicine measures, and the rapid acquisition of industrial skills.[24] In the context of national unity, the churches have built ecclesiastical structures that straddle the different ethnic groups and give church members a sense of belonging together in a national way. Strangely enough also, some small contribution to political pluralism and democracy springs from Christian differences: democracy at its best requires that political splits should not follow social cleavages too closely, and in a country like Nigeria, where the

24. J. K. Galbraith has written: ". . . a dollar or a rupee invested in the intellectual improvement of human beings will often bring a greater increase in national income than a dollar or a rupee devoted to railways, dams, machine tools, or other tangible capital goods. To rescue farmers and workers from illiteracy may certainly be a goal in itself. But it is also the first indispensable step to any form of agricultural progress. Nowhere in the world is there an illiterate peasantry that is progressive. Education, so viewed, becomes a highly productive form of investment." *Economic Development in Perspective* (Cambridge, Mass., 1962), p. 49.

main political parties have tended to organize along ethnic lines, there has been some value in Ibo Catholics, for example, finding themselves on the same religious side as Yoruba Catholics to whom they and Ibo Protestants would be politically opposed.

2. Modernization and not Westernization

a. Many of the changes that have taken place in Africa— though they have come about through contact with Western ideas and organizational forms and the machines that the Westerners brought with them—have meant much less the Westernization of Africa than its modernization. Ideas such as those of mathematics and inventions such as machines belong exclusively to no one culture. Once discovered or invented, they belong by right to all mankind. Moreover, once the ideas or the machines arrive, they bring their own logic with them. The pre-Newtonian cosmologies and the social structures of traditional African societies were bound to be profoundly modified once the analytico-causal attitude of modern science came in and the machines began to turn in the countryside. Those Africans who run the administration —like the missionaries before them—have discovered that some things traditional had to go if their countries are to enter the modern world. Land tenure, for example, needs to be reformed in many districts if farm production is to be increased; ingrained notions about childbirth must be eradicated if infant mortality is to be reduced; a leisurely and approximate approach to time must give way to greater precision if industrialization is to be successful. In other words, African traditions like all great traditions have to purify themselves incessantly so as to survive and grow.[25]

b. To imply—as has just been done—that Christianity as

25. I have written elsewhere on the specificity of African culture in relation to universalizing influences that affect a particular culture through modern science and technology: see "The Clash of World Civilization and Individual Cultures," *Ibadan*, XIV (October, 1962), 3-7.

a factor of modernization could not help destroying elements of tradition is a negative contention. More important is the fact that Christianity brought certain positive attitudes and ideas with it. Once the scientific outlook had taken root and technological achievement had got under way, many facets of the old religious culture were doomed. Science has, for instance, desacralized the storm. A storm is now a series of physical events: barometers, thermometers, and telescopes have eliminated Shango, the Yoruba storm god. Similarly, modern medicine has killed Shonponna, the smallpox god. But the gods were the face of the Absolute and channeled divine power to men. What Christianity has been able to do is to give new significance to the West African high god. Had this not happened, great sections of African peoples, inheritors of strong religious traditions, would have had to live despoiled of religion, without forms of worship and without convictions as to the source of existence and a knowledge of where they had come from and were going to.

Modern scientific attitudes are based essentially on an acceptance of predictability which derives from uniformities found and sought in both the physical and (in a different way because freedom enters into play) human worlds. Christianity which itself accepts a desacralized world, created by God with its own laws, fosters the growth of a scientific attitude among its African adherents. Not the least important part of its influence in this respect is to offer a social structure that transcends those bonds that have been traditionally meaningful—ethnic community, family loyalty, linguistic identification—and enables people to enter into relationships of predictability based on rational knowledge and trust with people from different social categories. In countries committed to economic growth, this Christian mental effect is quite important because scholars have come more and more to realize that "social attitudes constituting an impediment to economic change"[26] are more serious than the absence of capital or physical resources or even skills. Indeed, finally, we might point out that Christianity has accustomed people to change that has not been completely socially disruptive. Indeed, it has helped in important ways in the transitional West African societies to mitigate tensions through its religious doctrine, community organization, and welfare measures.[27]

c. Technology makes possible, and even tends to create, large-scale groupings. Also, through its communication systems, it makes men conscious of ideas of truth and values held by communities other than their own. The days of the small religious communities with a form of anthropological religion and creation myths proper to themselves have gone. People have gradually grown to understand that religious truth, like all truths, knows no boundaries and belongs to no one people. The universalism of Christianity matches the universalism of scientific thought. In spite of isolated attempts to relapse into a parochial isolation, Africans realize that they are now committed to and belong to a world system.

3. *Number and devotion of Christians*

Over the years Christians have built up loyal communities that more and more are served by African priests. It is not

26. Heilbroner, *op. cit.*, p. 47.

27. Milton J. Esman in an unpublished paper, "The Politics of Development Administration," writes: "Persons involved in any process of rapid change tend to feel adrift. The major values, institutions and behavior patterns which provided security and predictability are rapidly eroding; new patterns have not clearly emerged to replace them and to provide the focus of integration for the individual. Such phenomena as alienation, anomie, crises of identity, self-hatred, and other symptoms of psychological disintegration appear on a large scale. These symptoms are characteristic of transitional societies, and tend to be magnified by the economic dependency which accompanies urbanization, technological change, and the breakdown of kinship institutions. Mitigating these tensions through community organization, welfare measures, and doctrine which conveys a sense of stable purpose can reduce the possibility of social and political disturbance, enhance individual and group productivity, and foster the integration of the individual into modern roles and institutions."

easy at this stage to call into question the patriotism of these people. Moreover, more than most other groups they have taken part in the process of social mobilization and wield an influence out of proportion to their numbers. A vast section of the intelligentsia owes its formation to mission schools. It is significant that in Western Nigeria after a state of emergency had been declared in May, 1962, the administrator appointed by the federal government to take over (while the regional government was suspended) went ostentatiously to church at St. James Anglican Cathedral at Ibadan as part of the public process of legitimizing his rule.

Conclusion

The relative good will that at present exists between church and state in West Africa has a positive and negative basis. Negatively the political leaders have not seen the power and the influence of churchmen as a challenge to themselves (apart from the initial but quickly dropped resistance to the nationalist movement) and the churchmen have not found the political leaders unduly hostile in spite of the extreme declarations that some of them have made from time to time exalting the power of the state or the role of the party. Positively the governments have been willing to have the churches collaborate in the tasks of socioeconomic modernization and to let them go ahead with their spiritual mission. Moreover, good relations owe a lot to the fact that so many politicians have received at least part of their education in mission schools and that many of them are linked in friendship with religious leaders.[28] Those tensions that have arisen so far have come from the slowness of the Christian churches to remove all basis from accusations of foreignness and from an involvement in the sphere of education. But the tensions

28. Either the head of government or the chief executive in Senegal, Sierra Leone, Ivory Coast, Liberia, Upper Volta, Togo, Dahomey, and Nigeria professes Christianity as his religion.

have been notably less important than the general good relations.

Indeed what churchmen may have to be most on their guard against in the years immediately ahead is less hostility from the contemporary generation of political leaders than excessive identification with them and the present social order which holds elements of injustice and instability. The civil authorities will expect ecclesiastical support in their effort to maintain the established political order. Yet it is important to distinguish two facets of the ruling elite in West Africa: (*1*) They are statesmen who are genuinely concerned with national unity, economic growth, and social welfare and who seek to organize the energies of their peoples to achieve these goals. (*2*) They are politicians who have wrested power from the colonial authorities and who have no intention of losing that power to other politicians. They have not hesitated to use ruthless measures to prevent or suppress opposition. It is possible to sympathize with governments that, faced with well-nigh impossible developmental tasks, use forceful measures to prevent opposition parties or factions from whipping up discontent with policies that the country needs but that are not going to be easily understood by the populace. Yet it is also true that an inefficient and corrupt regime will plead the national interest as an excuse to eliminate the opposition and hang on indefinitely to power. In practice few regimes are either thoroughly efficient and incorrupt or the opposite. So the church is likely to find herself co-operating with many projects and obeying in the temporal sphere governments that are mixed in their elements of good and evil. Churchmen will have much to gain from not being identified with particular regimes or forms of government. Above all, they must not allow themselves to become associated with those aspects of injustice that characterize a regime. And they need to avoid interference in the purely temporal sphere where their maneuverings will be resented and where they have no right to decide that Christian moral teaching favors one or the other of the many technical solutions that difficult and complex socioeconomic problems call for. The most important contribution that the church can make towards solving these problems is to work to awaken that awareness of the love and justice of God in men's hearts that makes them solicitous for the good of their fellows.

Even if the African countries have political leaders that are both efficient and upright, there is no guarantee that they can implement social policies and make use of technical advice given by groups ranging from economists and sociologists to engineers and agronomists in such a way as to satisfy in the immediate future the aspirations that have already been awakened. Political tensions will be inevitable—they may even provide an important part of the social dynamism that urges leaders along—and stability at the best of times may be problematical. But in the actually existing situation where the balance of power between opposing political parties (or factions within the one-party systems) is open to change as development takes place; where ruling groups enjoy an uneasy legitimacy and can only make use of an imperfect constitutionalism; where important sections of the leadership are incompetent and corrupt; where regimes that had secured the transfer of power before a better educated intelligentsia arrived on the scene have alienated the majority of the latter group; where a growing awareness of deprivation exists among town proletariats and unemployed school-leavers—political instability rather than stability is the most likely future. Under such circumstances the churches have everything to gain by realizing that though justice is a concern for them, they are not committed to supporting any one political group or to promoting any one set of technical solutions. If they link themselves to a political group or to a set of technical solutions, they do so against the logic of their spiritual

doctrine and at great practical peril to their continuing freedom of action.

In these developing states—to return to a theme that we
began with in our introductory section—governments are
going to require great powers to cope with the immense tasks
that groups other than governments can do little to cope with
effectively. Because governments will need great powers, they
may be tempted to arrogate all powers to themselves and to
deny the legitimacy of groups that do not come under complete state control. That totalitarian attitude—should it come
to exist—would ignore the administrative possibilities of the
new governments. It would also ignore the human issues of
individual identity, social worship of God, and ultimate destiny that transcend the political order and belong to the
sphere of organized religion. If totalitarian solutions are seriously propounded or attempted, the churches will abdicate
their mission unless they speak out or resist. A fear to test the
loyalty of their members in a joust with the power of the
state would reduce them to a whimpering ineffectiveness
even in their purely religious mission. A faith in God that
dared not confront Caesar would ill fit Christian doctrine or
tradition. Yet on the other hand clerics must be prepared for
a heavy socializing future and not cry "wolf" too soon should
the state impose its planning, whether in education or in any
other sphere. In any case the churches must concern themselves principally with the spiritual mission that confronts
them directly: to evangelize millions of pagans, to deepen the
faith of existing Christians, to Africanize the expressions of
doctrine and forms of worship, and to recruit more, and train
better, candidates for the clergy.

For quite some time to come the Christian churches—and
alongside them various Muslim groups—are likely to be the
most effective groups to demonstrate that though all groups
in a state are subject to political conditioning and some political direction, not all groups are completely subject to

political control. Human society needs a political structuring. But life is richer and wider than politics. Some social diversity and freedom, which is what pluralism means, are basic to a proper living of human life. Diversity and freedom generate that manifold personal spontaneity through which initiative, whether in art or religion or economic entrepreneurship, flourishes. It is in this context that we must understand the importance of the relations that are worked out beween church and state in West Africa.

Appendix

Religious Affiliations in West African Countries

Country	Population total	Catholics	Protestants	Muslims	Animists
Cameroun	3,873,548	776,972		605,379	
Dahomey	1,756,000	238,148	17,600	123,000	1,341,000
Gambia	280,500	4,451	3,500	214,000	58,000
Ghana	6,690,730	562,912	686,000	687,000	4,658,133
Guinea	2,727,000	25,110	1,000	1,700,000	1,000,000
Portugese Guinea	550,000	15,000		165,000	320,000
Spanish Guinea	240,000	192,731		950	65,000
Ivory Coast	3,240,000	235,836	69,574	678,455	2,193,237
Liberia	1,500,000	12,804	60,000	250,000	1,176,000
Mali	3,745,875	18,607	1,962	2,331,150	1,383,399
Mauritania	730,000	2,678		721,000	
Niger	2,600,000	10,600	579	1,800,000	727,547
Nigeria	34,443,000	1,750,000	1,030,000	15,090,000	15,870,000
Senegal	2,260,000	143,225	900	1,633,500	474,428
Sierra Leone	2,300,000	18,545	70,000	800,000	1,400,000
Togo	1,116,000	205,226	42,807		780,000
Upper Volta	3,884,000	131,343	9,274	995,500	2,698,000

These figures are given in *Ready Information about Africa* (London: Mission Information Centre, St. Edward's College, 1962). They can be taken as approximative only.

RELIGIOUS DEVELOPMENTS
IN AFRICA

G. McLeod Bryan

When "Zik" (Dr. Azikiwe, currently the first governor-general of Nigeria) was campaigning for the premiership in the 1959 independence elections, one village welcomed him with four ceremonial gifts: a Bible ("to revere Jehovah"), a Koran ("to honor Allah"), a white rooster ("to sacrifice to the tribal god"), and a sword ("to hack his way to victory over his enemies"). These gifts typify the religious complexity of Africa south of the Sahara, a region which promises to be the world's best laboratory in which to observe religious pluralism.

Not all the world's classic religions are involved in the tryst that is new Africa, but the continent does exhibit a cross-section of the liveliest alternatives in contemporary religions. First, there are the endless variations of the Islamic and Christian missionary penetration, the latter largely fashioned after its imported forms from abroad. Breaking away from the latter, indigenous Christianity, weak and struggling under limited leadership, is trying to reassert itself in an adaptation of African structures under the genius of the faith. Further diffusion occurs in the multitude of cults which mix elements of Christianity, Islam, and tribal religions in a peculiar syncretism. Alongside these is the resuscitation of the tribal gods under the self-conscious attempt to establish "the African Personality." Finally, there is the makeshift fabrication of the utilitarian political religions, including, of course, the live option of communism. In the rapid social change stirring Africa, religion—instead of being a steadying, cohesive influence—is apparently as shaken and transformed as any other social institution.

Until the decolonization and nation-building of this decade, the religious structure of Africa was regarded as experiencing an orderly transformation. Under colonial occupation Africans were being detribalized at a constantly increasing rate and were being absorbed into the mission churches at a ratio far exceeding that in the non-Western world. It was expected that Africans would soon move on a one-way street "from cannibalism to Christianity." Islam was considered no threat, since it was thought to be well contained by military borders, and as late as mid-twentieth century an appraisal in an international Protestant journal spoke of it as "moribund." The secular religions of Europe had not yet entered the contest for loyalties in Africa, and little was known by Africans of the techniques by which a political religion can be useful in the building of a nation-state. Tribal religions were considered (except by some anthropologists) to be not only fruitless, but actually harmful: so "heathenish" as to invite brutal replacement by the "superior" religion of the occupying foreign powers.

Suddenly, as though exploded by a time bomb, this picture of African religious life has been shattered. Christianity, it now appears—in spite of its enforced status as the privileged religion of the conquering powers, by which it wrested favorite lands for mission settlements—handled most of the education and health facilities for the continent, even sometimes profited from trading, and worked often hand-in-glove with the colonial officers to select and pacify the native leaders; in spite of its widespread geographical dispersion and numerical accumulations of membership, Christianity is but a thin veneer. Often the Africans proved themselves smarter than their "converters" by simply adapting themselves overtly to the pattern of their mentors, while covertly retaining their own basic allegiances. Moreover, the Christianity that was introduced was too weakened by the internal divisiveness of its imported Western forms, divisiveness linked not only to the major conflict between Roman Catholicism and Protestantism, but also existing between denominations attached to the various nations of the West as well as obtaining within denominations exported from the same country. As a consequence Africa has probably more sects and cults than any other continent. Once transplanted, the African genius for further adaptation went to work, and the indigenous Christianity of Africa has become the most splintered of any in the world. In spite of belated and feeble movements toward ecumenicity represented by the newly formed Christian councils, the Christian religion is not one formidable institution for good in Africa, any more than it has been in other parts of the world. Subsequently we shall call attention to the fact that many Christians throughout the African continent, both missionaries and nationals, are well aware of these shortcomings and are making haste to overcome them. Suffice it to say now that the one inescapable fact of the future for Christianity in Africa is that it must be prepared for an entirely new era, one in which it faces its sternest challenge in this whirlpool of sects and ideologies.

I. *Islam*

As the curtain rises on developing Africa, Islam is on the offensive. But even behind the closed curtains of colonial occupation it could already be seen as the most Pan-African force on the continent. Islam might quite properly be called the religion of Africa, if one takes this to mean the one religious loyalty which unifies more people under a common rite and ethic. All who quote bits of the Koran, all who pray toward Mecca, all who observe Ramadan are world brothers, and all who have made the Pilgrimage are honored brothers. This holds true not merely for North Africa, but for the belt of the continent as well, where if twenty-five countries were numbered among the independent today, twenty of them would tomorrow undoubtedly be Moslem-dominated on the basis of universal suffrage and one-party democracy.

The leaders of Islam recognize that this is a crucial moment in Africa's history and are making new bids for power and numbers. Young Moslems, indoctrinated in Cairo and Khartoum and intoxicated with the Pan-Arabic, Pan-Islamic dream, are busily pushing their demands amidst the changing power-structures of governments. Missionaries from faraway Pakistan, especially of the Ahmadiyya sect, and from the Ishmaeli sect on the East Coast, provide a necessary outside stimulus. All the way to Capetown this is the case. Radio and newspapers have been substituted for the sword and steed. Schools and liberalized mosques are recruiting stations and replace patriarchal fiat. More and more youths are acknowledging allegiance to the Moslem faith, and on university campuses they are vigorously defending their beliefs and demanding equal representation in the curriculum and chapel life.

These modern strategies augment the older advantages of Islam: namely, that the trading languages of much of West, Central, and East Africa—Swahili and Hausa—are also those of the faith; that the Moslem proselytizer comes as one African to another; that the Moslems do not separate themselves from the villagers but share the same standard of living; that Islam is free of racism and more easily adapts its religious rites to local customs; and that the history of Islamic people's exploiting Africa is not as fresh in the minds of Africans as is the imperialism of the West.

Moreover, governments which are sympathetic to the Moslem religion, though not necessarily approving its theocratic politics, are turning the tables on Christian missionary power. Already Christian missionaries have been deported from Guinea, Sudan, and Somaliland. The Emirs of Nigeria, whose power represents numerically the majority of this most populous country of Africa and from whose ranks comes its present premier, once declared: "Holding this country together is not possible except by means of the religion of the Prophet. . . . If they [all other political factions] want political unity let them follow our religion." But above and beyond all these factors it can be said that Islam is capturing the imagination of Africans largely because, in the confusion of the moment when multifragmented Christianity is more and more considered a foreign religion of the whites and bears the incubus of colonialism, it offers a simplified answer to national unity.

But Islam does have certain impediments in ministering to emerging Africa. The Koran which must be studied in Arabic and the prayers which must be said in Arabic are known to the African only by memory, repetition of which is often pure jibberish as their profound meanings frequently escape the one who prays by rote. Moreover, Islam covered the African continent in the days before modern transportation and mass communication, without the humanitarian persuasion of schools and hospitals and respect for feminine rights. The big question now is whether, when nearly all Africans are demanding these as common necessities, Islam can modernize itself fast enough.

In its encounter with Christianity, Islam is more resistant than the tribal religions. Yet the record of coexistence of Islam and Christianity is better in Africa south of the Sahara than anywhere else in the world. Significant "conversations" are occurring among leading representatives of both faiths, such as the Asmara conference in Ethiopia in 1959 and with the two full-time consultants the Christian councils employ in West Africa. In its encounter with tribalism, Islam blends easily at the daily level of communal solidarity and mystic symbolism; yet in its developed theology it is unalterably opposed to idolatry and polytheism and imposes stringent moral demands and a universalism which inevitably undermines narrow-minded tribalism. It is not readily amenable to the freshly fabricated nationalistic religions since its own theocratic aspirations move in an opposite direction. It is held to be a major barrier against the introduction of communism to Africa.

We can safely conclude that Islam is deeply rooted, is vigorously refurbishing itself in the competition for the African mind, and if it can overcome its traditionalist elements which tend to set it over against the scientific, technological, and humanitarian movements in the modern world, it may well maintain its phenomenal growth. On the other hand, its present prosperity may mean that it is little more than a convenient middle stage for the African breaking away from animistic tribal religions on the way to a liberation which in turn will lead to something now wholly unpredictable.

II. *Tribal Religions*

While it appears that tribalism in Africa has been dealt a deathblow by the multiple innovations, this is not to say that tribalism will disappear at once. Bleak as its future may be, the latest anthropological judgment agrees that: "Despite the intensity of Christian missionary effort and the thousand years of Moslem proselytizing which have marked the history of various parts of Africa, African religions continue to manifest vitality everywhere."[1] Its recrudescence is due in part to its own resiliency in the face of invading pressures, in part to the desire of the new political elites of Africa for a native religious mystique to undergird their "Négritude" and "Pan-African" propaganda, and in part to a genu-

1. William Bascom and Melville J. Herskovits, *Continuity and Change in African Culture* (Chicago, 1959), p. 3.

ine reassessment of the integrity of tribal religions. Some have come to understand the religious practices of a preliterate people, not as a disorderly set of superstitions and destructive habits (which might be straightened out in a hurry by anyone with a white skin), but rather as a framework for integrating and sustaining institutions, roles, symbols, and ethos among its adherents. "Primitive religion," writes Harvard anthropologist William Howells, "is not a name for childish tumult and bestial abandon. It is careful, thoughtful, purposeful; and it is good medicine. Primitive people have long ago put into practical religious forms many things that your countrymen are trying to find for themselves in lectures and books on the good society, or on how to find happiness, or on what is wrong with them. This is not because the Noble Savage is so exceedingly noble; it is just that his religions are meaningful, and we can learn something from them."[2]

Yet not everything is good in these primitive religions. They, like the garden varieties of so-called higher religions, have exhibited both socially cohesive, psychic values, and anti-social practices. No doubt the survival value, the integrity, and the benefits of African tribalism depend greatly upon the importance of religions of the socially cohesive type. At the same time, the preponderance of antisocial elements must be acknowledged: the fear of witches, the use of black magic, the loss of life through initiation ceremonies, the practice of erratic divination for personal and social decisions, and the dependence upon emotionally unstable leaders.

Few things in Africa are being more radically revised than the conception of the positive role of religion in the ordinary African's life. Religion for him is all-embracing. "From conception to death, from morning till night, from springtime until harvest, and from the start of any enterprise (whether building a house or hunting for hippos) until its end, super-

2. William Howells, "The Primitive World," *Wisdom* (Feb., 1956), p. 45.

natural forces are present and must be properly dealt with, or failure is inevitable."[3] Naturally, where the least reflection about this process occurs—and it occurs rarely because thinking rationally about one's religion is a rare phenomenon— it is likely to be rationalized. However, there are significant beginnings. President Nkrumah of Ghana has ordered the religion department of his national university to include the study of tribal religions on a par with Christianity and Islam. The brochure that opened the first African-initiated seminar on "West African Religion," held at the Nigerian University at Ibadan, December, 1959, reads:

There is no aspect of West African Culture that is more misunderstood and misrepresented than West African forms of Religion. Almost every word in the English language that is commonly used to describe African Religion is a term of abuse. . . . Since then our views have greatly changed. Many manifestations of African culture are now accepted as important contributions to world culture: African art, drumming and dancing for example. Yet the very Religion that inspired African art and music is still subjected to the same form of prejudices. In this course an attempt is being made to discuss West African society and government, the part it played in the evolution of the African personality, the ethical values it represents and its relationship to Christianity.

Simultaneously, Fourah Bay College in the West and Makerere College in the East were encouraging the serious study of tribal religion. The latter sponsored extramural lectures in 1958 on "Religion and Society in East Africa" (later published), and the former initiated the *Sierra Leone Bulletin of Religion,* the first issue of which announced: "This is an attempt to provide a means of collecting and sifting information on the forms and history of religion, both Christian and non-Christian, within one fairly compact African territory."

The key, perhaps, to the future of religion in Africa, is the fact that in spite of what we have been led to believe by the

3. Eugene Nida and William Smalley, *Introducing Animism* (New York, 1959), p. 55.

reports of missionaries which depreciated the value and influence of native religions on the lives of Africans, most Africans
have not wholly capitulated to the Western world's denigra-
tion of the spiritual. The spiritual realm is still decisive if not
primary for them. Significantly, no new nation-state has declared itself officially for atheism. That the African does not
dismiss spiritual considerations is all the more clear now that
learned Africans are articulating their own social aspirations.
For instance, in the recent analysis of the problems facing his
countrymen, *The African Nations and World Solidarity,*
Mamadou Dia, Prime Minister of Senegal, turns away from
both capitalism and communism because both have succeeded
"at the sacrifice of religion, of the soul." Again, Juluis
Nyerere, President of Tanganyika, recommends a third way
between the Western and Eastern blocs, a way which includes
the spiritual values of "communitarianism," to use his term.
Many other leaders, prominent among whom are Northern
Rhodesia's Kenneth Kaunda and South Africa's Albert Luthuli, unashamedly rest their case for the future development
of Africa on the spiritual factor in a way which is embarrassing to modern Westerners.

The radically revised evaluation of the effect of tribal religions on Africans, as over against the distorted reports of
nineteenth-century missionaries who so often viewed them
from behind the blinders of Victorian Puritanism and scientific rationalism, may be discovered in the contrast between
what the venerable missionary Robert Moffat recorded in his
journal about the Bechuanas among whom he labored for
half a century, and Prof. E. B. Idowu of the University of
Nigeria writing currently about his own Yoruba people.
Allowing for the wide divergence between two cultures so
distantly separated, one immediately discerns a basic difference in initial appreciation. Moffat held that "The Bechuanas had really no conscience until it was formed by the missionaries." He refers to them as "rude and savage men, bar-

barians," whose "only gods are meat and tobacco." As he looked over his mission at the close of his career he was joyously surprised since he had known most of them "in their naked, wild heathen state" and now beheld them "clothed and in their right mind."[4] Idowu reports that

the keynote of (Yoruba) life is their religion. In all things, they are religious. Religion forms the foundation and the all-governing principle of life for them. As far as they are concerned, the full responsibility for all the affairs of life belongs to the Deity. ... The religion of the Yoruba permeates their lives so much that it expresses itself in multifarious ways. It forms the theme of songs, makes topics for minstrelsy, finds vehicles in myths, folktales, proverbs and sayings, and is the basis of philosophy.[5]

Both of these reporters are Christians; could it be that the difference in their reporting lies in the fact that one is a nineteenth-century outsider, and the other is a twentieth-century insider?

Still the reservation remains: will the largely static and local tribal religions, badly shaken by the innovations from without and seriously questioned by the young Africans from within, be able to bear the expectations placed upon them by the Neo-African romanticists, on the one hand, and the politicians who would convert them into utilitarian religions, on the other? The answer is already in hand for the politically obsessed Africans: they demand a religious mystique more readily amenable to their nationalistic and Pan-African goals. Their appeal to "the gods of Africa" is not necessarily a genuine reversion to their tribal gods. African politicians as entrenched and strongminded as President Nkhrumah of Ghana and Emperor Haile Selassie of Ethiopia have discovered that local religious leaders can be formidable obstructionists to national policy. Moreover, all observers of religions know that narrow religious loyalties can divide not

4. Cecil Northcott, *Robert Moffat* (New York, 1961), p. 70.
5. E. Bolaji Idowu, *Olodumare: God in Yoruba Belief* (London, 1962), p. 379.

only those of the same race, but can make bitter enemies of neighbors. In other words, there is considerable doubt that a romantic appeal to "the gods of Africa" can elicit the spiritual motivation necessary to the building of a community of nations in Africa.

III. *Political Religions*

Perhaps for that reason tribal religions are being reshaped by political leaders for their own ends, and are being merged with elements from Islam and Christianity to form a cultic syncretism which can either be utilized by the romantic and political Pan-Africanists or provide the psychic support for the hordes of mobile, urbanized Africans uprooted from their tribal moorings. For instance, President Nkrumah had his tribal priests pour a libation at the airport reception for the Queen of England. And it is rumored that he consults tribal divinators, whether as a devout believer or for political advantage remains unknown.

The motto, "Seek ye first the political kingdom and all other things shall be added unto it"—the words inscribed at the base of the Kwame Nkrumah statue in front of the Parliament in Accra—is the foundation of the new political religion. Toynbee has observed that "for the moment in Africa nationalism has supplanted the nominal (traditional) religions in fact, though not avowedly."[6] For many it has become a new religion, a substitute for the old tribal loyalties and a live option to Christianity and Islam. African nationalism has its high priests, its saviors, its prophets; it has its ritual, its hymns, its mythos; it has its pilgrimages and rallies. In fact, it has all the manifestations of political messianism. Christians in Ghana, for instance, have been horrified at the blasphemy implicit in references to the President as "Savior," at

6. A. J. Toynbee, "Will Nationalism Destroy Mankind?" *Winston Salem Journal,* Jan. 19, 1960, p. 4.

the substitution of political lines in traditional hymns, and at the rise of organizations patterned after the church and its liturgy. The Anglican Bishop Richard Roseveare of Accra accused the government-sponsored youth organization, Young Pioneers, of being "godless" (they sang, "Nkrumah does no wrong" and "Nkrumah will never die") and was promptly expelled on August 13, 1962. Since then he has been welcomed back by a special dispensation from his old friend Nkrumah himself.

The larger aspects of this political religion, namely Pan-Africanism, make bold to transcend not only narrow national and tribal loyalties but also Christianity, Islam, and communism. Its "saint" was George Padmore, whose ashes are enshrined in the buttresses of Christianborg Castle. "Had I more than one life to live I would spend it for Africa," he wrote, for Pan-Africanism "offers an ideological alternative to Communism on the one hand and Tribalism on the other. It rejects both white racialism and black chauvinism. Pan-Africanism looks above the narrow confines of class, race, tribe and religion."[7]

IV. *Separatist Religions*

More indigenous, but also with political overtones, are the numerous cults which have mushroomed throughout the whole continent, arising from the grass roots with altogether local leadership. Typical of these cults which blend elements of tribal religions, Christianity, and Islam are such diverse movements as the Kimbangu sect in the Congo, the Alice Movement in Northern Rhodesia, the Shemba sect in South Africa, the Kikuyu sect (Watu wa Mngu: people of God) in Kenya, and the Cherabim and Seraphim in Nigeria. Several studies have been made of them, but the best are B. Sundkler's *Bantu Prophets* (revised edition, 1961), de Pury, *Les Eglises*

7. George Padmore, *Pan-Africanism or Communism?* (London, 1956), p. 379.

d'Afrique entre l'Evangile et la Coutume (1958), and F. B. Welbouran, *East African Rebels* (1960). These studies together estimate over 2,000 such movements throughout Africa.

Each cult has a different origin, history, and ritual. For instance, the Congolese sect known as "The Church of Christ on Earth Through the Prophet Simon Kimbangu," flourishes anew since independence, in spite of the long-standing opposition of missions, under the leadership of Joseph Diangienda with a reported membership of 2,700,000. Diangienda is a son of Kimbangu, "a prophet who saw the light" in 1921 and began preaching what was described as "an African version of Protestantism." He was sentenced to death, but his sentence was commuted and he died in prison. Another son is Minister of Labor in the cabinet of Premier Adoula.

The "People of God" among the Kikuyu use the sacrifice of sheep and goats, the Protestant Bible, the Roman Catholic cross, and the Muslim habit of growing beards. They advocate a Black Christ and are fanatically anti-white, stirring up hatred that fanned the fires of Mau Mau. Kenyatta, returning to Kenya in 1946, founded more than three hundred schools among such disgruntled Kikuyu. These Kikuyu Independent Schools, as they were known, were mostly traditional in their religious allegiances and operated without the assistance of the government or of Europeans. When I interviewed the convicted Mau Mau leader, Jomo Kenyatta, when he was imprisoned in the ninth year of his enforced exile just before his release, I inquired about the Kenya government's suppressing these schools because they were teaching "barbaric and subversive" doctrines. He replied,

We merely taught that Christ was an African, that He belongs to Africa more than to other peoples of the world. No, we did not teach that He was black. We simply held that He learned His masterful wisdom during those most impressionable years when He was sheltered by Africans on His flight into Egypt. When he returned to Palestine, He was a unique combination of Judaeo-African religion.

That answer seems to represent the general motive for and the spirit of these sects, other than the purely human ambitions of the founders. They combine an intense resentment against the whites for having ignored them and a strong attachment to the faith and culture of their fathers with vestiges of the Christian faith they have picked up in elementary Bible classes and church services they have attended. The political potential of the separatists is easy to see. What developed was "Ethiopianism," the label applied to the African's embryonic struggle for freedom as it grew within the bosom of the Church. ("Ethiopia" because of the Scripture reference, "Ethiopia shall soon stretch out her hands unto God," Psalm 68:31, and because of the rising African consciousness of this ancient monarchy possessing a national church with a tradition older than many European ones.) The beginnings of the movement lie in obscurity, but the mood is a continent-wide one. A South African historian records:

It is an interesting fact that the first Bantu mass movement on truly national lines was a religious one. What came to be called Ethiopianism was an attempt on the part of Christian Africans to set up their own churches independent of white ones. . . . Though outwardly religious, they were to a large extent political in their appeal. They began as a revolt of the black members within the missionary churches.[8]

A more recent study has concluded that where "missionary conservatism was perhaps most pronounced and where the problem was often aggravated by color prejudice, it was an important factor in protest against the combination of mission and colonial domination."[9] Welbourn concludes, "There is in fact every evidence that African movements toward independence start with independent churches and end

8. Edward Roux, *Time Longer Than Rope* (London, 1949), p. 85.
9. Paul Abrecht, *The Churches and Rapid Social Change* (London, 1961), p. 88.

in a self-conscious nationalism with its total rejection of European leadership."[10]

A recent episode in the continuing history of the strained relations that have developed between the separatist Christianity of the Africans and the mission churches illustrates the exactly opposite attitudes taken by the two respective groups in Kenya with reference to Kenyatta's release. Significantly, the African church leaders in official session (April, 1961) unanimously demanded his immediate release and in so doing constituted the first major segment of Kenya society to ask for his release. The European reaction was immediate. Kenya's most prominent Presbyterian pastor, then attending the General Assembly of the Church of Scotland in Edinburgh, attacked the suggestion: "Our people in Kenya have greeted with incredulity the suggestion that Kenyatta should be released. . . . (he is) demoniac and satanic, and many people are still in his evil grip. This man was responsible for untold misery and the death of 15,000 of his own people, many Christians among them."[11] The Reverend Dr. Keltie's position was essentially that of a missionary who had reported as far back as 1949 that Kenyatta was assuming the role of a "black savior" and was leading his people away from Christianity and back to their tribal religion; his position was certainly no different from the Kenya governor's refusal to release Kenyatta because he was "the African leader to darkness and death." While the storm raged, six African church leaders visited Kenyatta in prison, and issued the following statement which was cosigned by the Anglican Bishop Obadiah and the African Presbyterian Moderator Kereri:

Contrary to our expectations we were impressed by his readiness to discuss religious matters. Surely, the return to normal life of the person we met in Maralal [his prison] does not terrify us. Jomo Kenyatta does not regard himself as God, neither does he

10. Quoted in *ibid.*, p. 88.
11. G. M. Bryan, "Kenya and Kenyatta," *The Christian Century,* LXXVIII (Aug. 9, 1961), 950-951.

claim any supernatural powers. He is a man, and it is for this man that we shall continue to pray, that he may come to a full knowledge of Jesus Christ.[12]

In August, 1962, he won his release.

Whether these schismatic religious movements will prosper, now that national independence is sweeping Africa, is questionable, especially since the policy of the mission boards is rapidly being changed to make all the African mission churches independent and to encourage African leadership in the Christian councils. (Until the time of the Congo crisis no Christian council in Africa was led by an African.) Indicative of the new epoch is the number of indigenous African churches which became new members of the World Council of Churches at its 1961 New Delhi Assembly: United Church of Central Africa in Rhodesia; Moravian Church in the Western Cape Province (South Africa); Union des Eglises Baptistes du Cameroun; Church of the Province of Uganda and Ruanda-Urundi; Presbyterian Church in the Cameroons; Eglise Evangelique du Gabon; Bantu Congregational Church (South Africa); Presbyterian Church of Nigeria; Evangelical Church of Northwestern Tanganyika; Eglise Evangelique Manianga Matado (Congo); Usambara-Digo Lutheran Church (Tanganyika).

Still almost nothing has been done to gather the multitudinous separatist sects into the ecumenical movement, if, indeed, they ever can be. However, the first major overture was made in 1962 when the All-Africa Church Conference Center at Mindola, Northern Rhodesia, staged a consultation to which separatist leaders from all over Africa were invited. They are by nature dissentious, are led for the most part by untrained leaders, and appeal to the masses of illiterate Africans who are bewildered by the new technological and political demands upon them. In the religious future of Africa, they can hardly be counted upon to contribute anything

12. *Ibid.*

positive unless they become something more than reactionary, isolated, self-interested splinter groups.

V. *Christianity*

Christianity in Africa, in spite of efforts to avoid division,
is sharply divided into two varieties: the prosperous Western
mission-dominated churches and the struggling indigenous
churches (the extreme varieties of which have just been described). On this division hinges the future of Christianity
in Africa in the immediate future. For there is a widespread
difference of opinion among the rising African leadership
about the merits of missionary Christianity, not only because
Christianity was often intimately associated with colonial exploitation, but because Christian missions still manifest too
much of a colonial and paternalistic attitude and policy.[13]

To understand this latter attitude we must keep in mind
that Africa is the most "missionized" spot on the globe, over
30,000 missionaries throughout the continent, over 10,000 in
the Congo alone. More than four hundred American church
organizations are involved in Africa. To this day, missionary
spending comprises a sizeable portion of the cash economy of
many villages; missionary housing occupies block after block
of the wealthiest, most desirable residences in cities like Lagos,
Leopoldville, and Accra; and missionary status symbols, including over-size automobiles and membership in plush
clubs, remind Africans of another side of their humanitarian
thrust. What to the American missionary seems normal (although it must be questioned whether he would ever live so

13. Cf. two recent studies which substantiate this: Peirce Weaver, *Ecumenical Beginnings in Protestant World Missions* (New York, 1963), and W. C.
Harr, *Frontiers of the Christian World Mission since 1938* (New York, 1962).
Weaver in his final chapter reveals that all is not well and with strong words
decries the unfortunate results of the "colonial mind," of "missionary imperialists," of "denominational imperialists." W. C. Harr, in chap. iv, speaks
of "Christian colonialism": "But that has happened in Africa too. It still
happens, we believe, in many areas." P. 104.

well at home on a clerical salary) is to the African just one more proof of his superior, condescending behavior. Add to that the fact that most missionaries are now engaged in a supervisory and/or financially administrative capacity to the African pastors and institutions and further evidence is available for the charge that African Christians are "simply lackeys to Western medicinemen."[14]

This reaction, especially from the political and intellectual elite, should not be underestimated. Whenever the new African articulates his impressions on this matter he invariably displays this attitude. The author has read nearly a hundred fictional and autobiographical works by Africans, and almost without exception they refer to "the ugly missionary." While, on the one hand, they may be lavish in their praise for the generous missionary assistance which laid the foundation for educational, medical, and political development, they nonetheless look with disfavor upon the imperialistic hold which the missionaries seem to have on many of their people.

Typical of these complaints is the recent autobiography of the first African to win the coveted Nobel Peace Prize, Zulu Chief Albert Luthuli's *Let My People Go*. Addressing himself to Westerners, he writes,

There's a tendency for your white missionaries among us to drift away—they sometimes get identified with the whites. . . . If this is true it has possibly come about because missionaries have too easily become "supervisors of Native Work" no longer identified with their people. . . . White paternalist Christianity—as though the white had invented the Christian Faith—estranges my people from Christ. Hypocrisy, double standards, and the identification of white skins wth Christianity, do the same.

Yet throughout the book he praises Christianity for rescuing

14. Cf. the conclusions of two Africans on this matter: John and Rena Karefa-Smart, *The Halting Kingdom* (New York, 1959). "Yet it is true that, with but few exceptions, missions have dominated the local churches and missionaries have formulated the policies and plans, while African pastors, teachers, and catechists have been engaged to work in a manner not much different from the employment of labor by the management of an industrial corporation." P. 67.

his family from static tribalism, for educating him in a world-view, for giving him a responsible political vocation. "Among my many debts to Adams [missionary college] . . . [was] that the Christian Faith is not a private affair without relevance to society. It was, rather, a belief which equipped us in a unique way to meet the challenges of our society."[15]

Tom Mboya, the young Kenyan politician at the forefront of Pan-African movements, was asked on a British Broadcasting Corporation interview August 18, 1960, his opinion on this question. He responded,

The image of Christianity in Africa has been tainted by the inability of missionaries to live up to what they have preached. There are exceptions, like Fr. Huddleston and Bishop Reeves and so on, but generally these people who preach Christianity have gone back in the evening to live in the select residential areas of the Europeans, they have gone back in some areas to worship in white churches, they have sent their children to white schools, they have gone to reserved European hotels and train accommodations. This has given a very bad impression of Christianity.[16]

What are the reasons for this seeming ingratitude? The good which Christianity has contributed to awakening Africa is universally known. Nigeria's governor-general Azikiwe summarized it most recently in August, 1962: "Through its evangelists and missionaries Christianity has played a leading role in the development of Africa's education, health and other social welfare services." The fact is that Christianity educated 90 per cent of all Africans until 1960, including the majority of its present political leaders; it established and manned most of the medical centers; it planted the seed of independence and constitutional democracy. As the 1945 Report of the British Royal Commission on Higher Education in West Africa declares:

When one looks for the root from which West African education sprang one comes back, everywhere and always, to the mission-

15. Albert Luthuli, *Let My People Go* (New York, 1962), p. 83.
16. Tom Mboya from a BBC interview, *The Listener* (Aug. 18, 1960).

aries. It was the Christian missions who first came out to the coast without desire for fee or reward. . . . It is a remarkable thing that even today, if the educational institutions conducted and supervised by the religious bodies were suddenly to vanish, the greater part of education in British West Africa would practically disappear.

But if Christianity has been the leading single factor for change in Africa during the last one hundred years, one can safely say that it is unlikely that it will play that role in the next one hundred years. The reasons are numerous. For one thing, the day of nineteenth-century foreign missions under the Livingstonian slogan, "Christianity, Commerce and Civilization (Western, that is)," is over. This is acknowledged both by Western experts in the mission field and by Africans as well.[17] Christianity introduced a revolution that ran roughshod over African institutions, but now that process is being curbed by better judgment within the mission movement and by barriers of resentment erected by Africans. The Nigerian novelist, Chinua Achebe, describes the end result in his book *Things Fall Apart* (1958):

The white man is very clever. He came quietly and peaceably with his religion. We were amused at his foolishness and allowed him to stay. Now he has won our brothers, and our clan can no longer act like one. He has put a knife on the things that held us together and we have fallen apart.[18]

Second, the initial eagerness of the African to imitate the white masters even in religion developed many "book-Christians," who simply adopted Christian names in order to secure

17. Cf. the judgment of the distinguished Dutch missionary scholar, Hendrik Kraemer, "The Missionary Implications of the End of Western Colonialism and the Collapse of Western Christendom," *History's Lessons for Tomorrow's Mission* (Geneva, 1960). "Now it must be stated with the strongest possible emphasis that in principle, though far from in fact, this whole [missionary] structure collapsed as a result of the second world war and its dramatic consequences. In this sense it is fully true that *'the era of missions has passed'*— *irrevocably* . . . Western colonialism has ended; therefore the missionary era of that period, which reflected the essential attitudes and structures of colonialism, has also ended." Pp. 202-203.

18. Chinua Achebe, *Things Fall Apart* (London, 1958), p. 158.

accompanying privileges, including education, travel, and clerical advancement. For them Christianity is but a veneer. Looking back over this period, anthropologists are divided in their judgment of how severe has been the displacement of African culture. While some anthropologists, like Geoffrey Gorer[19] and Jomo Kenyatta, have deplored the wrecking of tribal institutions and values by Christian missions, Dr. M. J. Field in her recently published field-studies in Ghana believes that this attack is unjustified. "Illiterate Africans have always been more shrewdly and critically reserved than either missionaries or anthropologists have suspected," she writes. "The naiveté has been on the part of the foreigner. Christianity has always been the object of invidious observation by African pagans though courtesy and concrete self-interest have often forbidden criticism to be outspoken."[20]

Third, Christianity has come to be identified almost entirely with white European Western culture. The older missionaries of the Livingstone era can hardly be expected to have thought otherwise. John Taylor, whose book, *Christianity and Politics in Africa*, is in part devoted to this problem, concludes, "There is not the slightest doubt that the great missionaries of the mid-nineteenth century had a profound conviction that colonial empire and Christianity were fully compatible."[21] Equally, present day Christianity has difficulty dissociating itself: "Too frequently the physical setting of Christian worship confirms this impression, with its church building adorned or encumbered (as you will) with the monuments, tablets and plaques which record a history that is in process of repudiation, or conceived in the architectural and liturgical terms dictated by English decorum and white

19. Cf. Geoffrey Gorer, *Africa Dances* (London, 1945). "I consider [missionary] influence in Africa is almost wholly deplorable. With possibly the best intentions they have made rogues out of honest men, selfseekers out of unselfish men, liars and perverts and neurotics out of men happily free from these defects." P. 152.
20. M. J. Field, *Search for Security* (London, 1960), p. 50.
21. John Taylor, *Christianity and Politics in Africa* (London, 1957), p. 91.

usage."[22] In spite of the fact that virtually all missionaries being sent out today have been informed and warned of this handicap, it is still the main impression that they give to Africans. A study in depth of African attitudes toward Christianity points out "how widespread is the simple belief that Jesus Christ was an European, was put to death by Europeans, and that his religion is for Europeans only."[23] More recently in the Sudan in January, 1963, nearly a hundred missionaries were expelled, in spite of the protest some of the foreign mission boards filed with the government: "We hope that the fact that Christianity is not a Western religion will enable the Sudanese government to reconsider its action on the basis of the fact that in their service to the people of Sudan the missionaries represent the worldwide Christian community."[24]

All of this evidence reveals the paradoxial role of Christianity in Africa. On the one hand, Christian missions have been largely responsible for the educational and medical provisions of the continent, yet because of their unavoidable involvement with colonialism and Westernization they are subject to being rejected. Again, Christianity introduced throughout the territory a universal humaneness and communication (putting most of the African languages into a printed alphabet for the first time); yet by virtue of its own internal divisions imported from abroad it introduced new forms of competition and intolerance on to African soil.[25] Moreover, even though there are signs of considerable loyalty to the Christian faith among some leaders and many of the rank-and-file, yet the indigenous churches are often unable to support themselves financially and are negligible in

22. Kenneth Cragg, "Africa: The Challenge of Islam," *The Christian Century*, LXXIX (February 7, 1962), 159.
23. John Taylor and Dorothea Lehmann, *Christians of the Copperbelt* (London, 1961), chaps. vii and viii.
24. Quoted in *The Christian Century*, LXXX (Jan. 2, 1963), 6.
25. In some countries the number of different missions is so great that the governments attempt to curb competition by banning mission stations within five miles of each other.

their own proselytizing. It appears that for a long time to come
they will need (and likely demand and enjoy) overseas financial and supervisory aid.[26] Again, whereas Christianity in
Africa did interpret itself in terms of social service (from the
time that Livingstone opposed the traffic in slavery), it was
concerned with health, education, and agriculture. Noticeably
absent, in retrospect, was its concern for training politicians,
journalists, and labor leaders. While today it still virtually
ignores the complicated problems posed by the mobility of
labor, the shortage of housing, the displacement of youths,
mass communications, in short, all of the problems accompanying newly urbanized life in a technological society. No
doubt, the social concerns of mission-Christianity merely reflect its own blatant shortcomings at home. At this point it
must be made clear that, in spite of the belated progress made
by some of the old-line mission boards operating in Africa,
the majority of Protestant missionaries in Africa belong to the
soul-saving evangelistic type who use medical care and education as a *means* to reaching a person spiritually. They believe
only in enough education to read the Bible (they distrust
higher education in their own life back home); they are
politically irresponsible and racially segregated at home; and
they are so sectarian as to believe that they alone have the
whole truth and are consequently unable to co-operate with
other Christian bodies. To these the Africans refer when they
speak of "the white bulls fighting on the fair soil of Africa"
or "the tyranny of the sectarians, with their loads of American money."

Such challenges as labor relations, youth work, recreation,
housing, an ethic of work, economic development, the population explosion, and mass communications are only just now
being heard. It is significant that President Nkrumah in Jan-

26. For example, when the Methodist Niger Conference was finally constituted in 1962 (from a mission which had begun 120 years previously as one
of the earliest in West Africa), there were 842 churches, 65,993 members, 57
missionaries, and 25 African ministers.

uary, 1963, called a private consultation with all the missions operating in Ghana and spurred them to contribute more directly to national development. The overall survey of these needs made recently by the World Council of Churches concludes that Christian concern in these areas seems "peripheral and slight, compared with the opportunities for action and service; the churches appear to be out of touch with the contemporary urban scene, and they are not responding to the dynamic challenge of the changing urban situation. . . . 'Consequently most of our mission program and methods appear to be utterly theoretical and irrelevant.' "[27]

Exceptions to this general neglect are the grass-roots consultations initiated by the World Council of Churches, through its "Rapid Social Change" survey beginning in 1959; the published studies such as "Changing Liberia, A Challenge to the Christian, 1959," "The Churches and Social Change in the Copperbelt of Northern Rhodesia, 1959," the standard of living study of Kenya, "The Social and Economic Conditions of Development, 1961," the South African Conference, 1959, "Christian Responsibility toward Areas of Rapid Social Change"; the statements of new political responsibility such as the study books, "Christian Responsibility in an Independent Nigeria, 1961" and "Kenya: Present and Future, 1959" by the respective Christian Councils; and finally the regular meetings staged throughout Africa by the All-Africa Church Conference (such as the All-Africa Christian Youth Assembly in Nairobi, January, 1963 and the Kampala Assembly, April, 1963), whose secretary resides at the Mindola Ecumenical Institute which itself operates a year-round center for research and lectures.

A major question about the role of Christianity in Africa centers about its contribution to political independence. In the present political whirlpool that is Africa, Christians are being compelled to become involved, sometimes ignorantly,

27. Abrecht, *op. cit.*, p. 151.

sometimes by default. That Christians have been delinquent in providing guidance for African nationalism is admitted. This admission issues from Christians themselves, not merely from the enemies of Christianity. Sithole, the young Rhodesian politician and preacher, comments in his book *African Nationalism*:

Let it be noted right from the outset that when the missionaries went to Africa, they had not the slightest idea of helping African nationalism as such. Their primary goal was to propagate the Gospel of Christ to their fellow human beings. The Church has been only a blind instrument in the whole process of African nationalism. On the whole, missionaries in Asia and Africa have been accused, and not without cause, of standing in the way of emerging nationalism. In the main, they have been staunch supporters of colonial rule so that colonial powers cannot blame the rise of African nationalism on the missionaries as a class.[28]

From the Secretary of the Christian Council of Kenya comes this personal letter:

I am afraid that political leaders everywhere have found the Churches reactionary. The more I think about this the more I feel it is not just the theological position. It is due mainly to the clash of generations, the missions and Churches really representing the old generation, whereas political leaders are, with few exceptions, relatively young. I have often been puzzled by the fact that the Church, which was in the vanguard of progress, enlightened thinking, etc., in the early periods of African development, and as such did win the confidence of all progressive elements within the old society, has failed in a large measure to render the same service to the second generation.

At the same time a West African writes:

My observation of the African scene leads me to conclude that the Christian Church is an extremely cautious institution as far as political issues are concerned. Pronouncements on political and socio-economic affairs at international and national conferences by church bodies tend to be so general and vague that they could not be of much help to the interested Christian politician, and if they are clear and direct they come too late to do much good. To be fair to the missionary church of Africa, I should add

28. Ndabamingi Sithole, *African Nationalism* (London, 1959), p. 51.

that this cautiousness is typical of Christian churches everywhere today.

Until now there has been too much silence on the part of mission churches; understandable, yes, but not entirely justifiable. Too often missionaries and even African church members remained aloof from freedom movements. Their loyalty to Christian principles, and to the church in which all are one in Christ was mixed with undue devotion to the status quo and to "things overseas." This tended to make them suspect to the ardent nationalist. It became the belief of many that the church opposed self-government. A writer from Central Africa summarized this reaction in a letter to the author: "An attitude of silence from the Church from overseas will always react in favor of its own national aspirations, and consequently an urge is given to the separatist tendency in the African mind, and the desire grows to see the Church reflecting the aspirations of the indigenous inhabitants." A local missionary writes: "The Church here tends to be very conservative and there is a feeling among the new generation that it is a museum altogether without justification." In the light of these random reports it is not surprising that a regional church conference concluded: "In the realm of modern politics and social life the influence of the Church has yet to be felt to a marked degree." The ablest authority on missions all over Africa is perhaps Max Warren of the Church Missionary Society, headquarters in London. He sustains the above conclusions:

The Church has laid very little store by its task of infiltrating the life of the State with men and women with the revolutionary fire of the Spirit in their lives. It has done even less to prepare Africans for an understanding of politics and the Christian's responsibility in and for politics. At a time when Africans are becoming more and more politically conscious, this represents a major failure on the part of the Church to exercise one of its functions in relation to the State. . . .

The Young African is going with knightly courage and hope,

but going, alas, without the inspiration of a vigil before God's altar, and the guidance and blessing of God's priest.[29]

Such is the record of the delinquency of Christianity with regard to rising African nationalism. Now that Africans are drunk with nationalism it is no more than natural that in her tipsy state some of them should accuse Christianity of neglect in fortifying her for her day of freedom. On the other hand, there are just as many observers, in fact some of the very critics cited above, who claim that Christianity planted the seed of independence. Where the Western churchmen represented free citizens in their own persons, where their mission schools educated in the concepts of freedom, where the Bible was allowed free interpretation, it was inevitable that the leaven of freedom should ferment.

First among these indirect benefits of Christianity was the Bible itself, which many claim is revolutionary enough. Men who share as widely divergent social views as Sir Philip Mitchell and Chester Bowles agree that this is the case. The former, who was the typical empire Britisher in his colonial office in Kenya for many years, wrote recently: "The Bible . . . I believe to have been the decisive force in the whole business . . . the prime mover [in the liberation of Africa]."[30] Chester Bowles, in a book summarizing his impressions, has said: "Thus the Christian missionaries and their Book have been in this very practical sense Africa's true revolutionaries."[31]

African leadership itself joins in this tribute to the influence of the Bible. Sithole raises and answers the question as follows:

What is the actual relevance of the Bible to African nationalism? . . . The Bible is redeeming the African individual from the power of superstition, individuality-crushing tradition, witchcraft, and other forces that do not make for progress. The same Bible is helping the African individual to reassert himself above colonial powers! It is inconceivable to a logical mind that the Bible could

29. M. A. C. Warren, *Caesar, The Beloved Enemy* (Chicago, 1955), p. 67.
30. From C. Grove Haines, ed., *Africa Today* (Baltimore, 1955), pp. 14-16.
31. Chester Bowles, *Africa's Challenge to America* (Berkeley, 1956), p. 104.

deliver the African from traditional domination without at the same time redeeming him from colonial domination.[32]

A second manifestation of the indirect contribution of Christianity to the development of Africa has been the education of her leaders. We have noted how virtually all of the politicians were educated in mission schools. Yet at the same time this was no guarantee that they would remain Christian in their lives and policies. Nonetheless, it can be expected that the friendships established, the loyalties formed, and the characters molded will have lasting effect.

Thomas Hodgkin maintains that the ideology underlying African nationalism is borrowed largely from Christianity. Foremost is the idea of "human brotherhood and the specifically Protestant conception of an 'Elect'; the traditional democratic belief in the 'right to choose our own governors, to cashier them for misconduct and to frame a government for ourselves.' "[33]

Third, bearing directly on the rise of African nationalism is the share missionaries and their home bases have contributed to "Ethiopianism," the label first applied to the African's embryonic struggle for freedom as it grew within the bosom of the church. As long ago as 1829, Robert A. Young published in New York An Ethiopian Manifesto, "Issued in defense of the Black Man's Rights, in the Scale of Universal Freedom." Apparently it did not take hold in Africa until the latter part of the nineteenth century when the splinter movement away from the established mission churches began. Subsequently, a series of apparently disconnected episodes in Africa's history stirred the seething pot of nationalism. Charles Domingo, a Nyasaland separatist, released a denunciatory pamphlet in 1910, reading in part:

The three combined bodies, Missionaries, Government and Companies, or gainers of money, do form the same rule to look upon

32. Sithole, op. cit., pp. 52-53.
33. Thomas Hodgkin, Nationalism in Colonial Africa (New York, 1956), p. 98.

the native with mockery eyes. It sometimes startles us to see that the three combined bodies are from Europe, and along with them there is a title 'Christendom' . . . we would advise them not to call themselves 'Christendom' but 'Europedom.' Therefore the life of the three combined bodies is altogether too cheaty, too thefty, too mockery.[34]

John Chilembwe, the first Nyasaland native to be educated in America and who helped Booth set up the ill-fated Providence Industrial Mission in 1901, led an uprising in 1915 to expel the Europeans. In the Congo, the Kimbangu fracas of 1921 resulted in the imprisonment of the revolutionary prophet who, according to one historian, had "excited his followers against authority . . . had even set himself up to be the Saviour of the Black Race and had called the white men his 'abominable enemy.' "[35] Such cases were infrequent but fairly widespread over the continent. For instance, about the same time, the United Native church, an offshoot of the English Baptist church in the French Cameroons, had "the whole town of Douala seething with religious 'revolt' in which natives paraded up and down the streets singing anti-European hymns." In Nigeria earlier, the United African church had seceded partly in protest against the British Church Missionary Society, whose first African Bishop, Crowther, was regarded as being too friendly to Europeans. Their constitution of 1891 said, "Resolved, that a purely Native African Church be founded for the evangelization and amelioration of our race, to be governed by Africans."

A more direct contribution of Christianity to African nationalism has been the intervention of missionaries and churches in liberation movements. All along there have been some missionaries who have pleaded for justice for the African and who sought to generate liberation movements. Space does not allow a complete listing of these heroic voices, but

34. George Shepperson, "The Politics of African Christian Separatist Movements," *African Affairs*, XXIV (July, 1954); *Independent Africa* (Edinburgh, 1958), pp. 163-164.
35. R. L. Buell, *The Native Problem in Africa* (New York, 1928), II, 605.

they include Dr. John Philip who was active in the early mission work of South Africa, Guy Clutton-Brock of St. Faith's Mission who was arrested during the Rhodesian emergency of 1959, and the Methodist mission's witness to the world in the Angola crisis of the sixties. The Church in South Africa is known the world over for its protests voiced by Father Trevor Huddleston (*Naught for Your Comfort*), the Rev. Mr. Michael Scott (*A Time to Speak*), Bishop Ambrose Reeves (*Shooting at Sharpville*), Alan Paton and Archbishop Joost de Blank. What is less well known is that leading churchmen in the Roman Catholic, Methodist, Congregational, Presbyterian, and even the Dutch Reformed churches have likewise made their conscience known.

Christianity, to conclude, does not have a clear record of positive benefits for Africans, nor can it be said that the new African is accepting Christianity uncritically. Christianity must be prepared for its crucial test as it encounters on an equal basis, without its former colonial prestige and burdened by its historical shortcomings, the other religions and ideologies in contemporary Africa. The revolt against everything European has certainly hurt the Christian cause although it may be hoped that this is a temporary swing of the pendulum. So has "the divided church," the "irrelevant gospel which prepares for another world while this one wastes away," "the snobbery of white culture which sees little good in African culture," "the separateness of the missionary in his compound, who follows nineteenth-century methods and is slow to give full responsibility to nationals." One could wish that the best of modern missionary strategy were being applied equally by all missions operating in Africa, a strategy described so ably by Bishop Stephen Neill as consisting of three stages: (*1*) the building up of indigenous churches; (*2*) the turning over of the leadership of these churches to native Africans and (*3*) this leadership turning to the world church for help in finishing the task not only of converting Africa but of the West as well. But as this essay has emphasized, this positive strategy prevails in only a small percentage of Christian activity in Africa.

Yet this kind of Christian activity does exist and is both effectual and influential. It may not as yet have produced an internationally known theologian but it does have its world servants. Foremost is the witness of Chief Albert Luthuli whose winning of the Nobel Peace Prize signifies an influence far beyond the borders of his own African independence movement. Among its world churchmen are Dr. Z. K. Matthews (formerly of Ft. Hare College, now in Geneva with the World Council of Churches); Dr. Donald M'Timkulu (formerly Secretary of the All-Africa Church Conference, now Director of Mindola Center); the first African Cardinal, Rugambwa of Tanganyika; Sir Francis Ibiam, governor-general of Eastern Nigeria and one of the presidents of the World Council of Churches; the Roman Catholic scholar, Abbé Alexis Kagame of Urundi; Professors Christian Baeta and K. A. Busia (now exiled) of Ghana; Dr. John Karefa-Smart, Minister of External Affairs of Sierra Leone, and Robert Gardiner, head of the U. N. Economic Development office for Africa. Christianity can count among its adherents political leaders like Kenneth Kaunda of Northern Rhodesia; Julius Nyerere of Tanganyika; Dr. G. Kiano of Kenya; President William Tubman of Liberia; President Sir Milton Margai of Sierra Leone and President Leopold Senghor of Senegal. Of the present twenty-three heads of independent African nations, sixteen received at least part of their education in Christian mission schools.

DEVELOPMENT: FOR WHAT?

Douglas V. Steere

In describing the process by which the people of the developing countries are moving into possession of the technological tools of our time, and of their being profoundly changed by this process, I am bound to be saying things that are perfectly obvious. But in doing this, I have been somewhat comforted and reassured by observing how frequently it is the case that the more obvious a thing is, the more readily it can be overlooked, and the area of development is no exception. The Dean of En Shems University in Cairo told me a story of a Russian collective farm which had a single control gate through which the workers had to pass in leaving or entering; a guard was present who examined them to prevent the stealing of any implements. Over a period of months, a peasant appeared at the gate each day with a wheelbarrow piled high with straw, and the guard poked around in it and, finding nothing, let him leave the farm. One day the guard told the peasant that he was to be transferred that night to a collective farm in another province and would therefore cause him no trouble, but before he left he would like very much to know what it was that he had been stealing. The peasant beamed and replied simply, "wheelbarrows."

Among these apparently obvious things in the technical assistance field is the central question I want to raise as to what we as the givers of aid are concerned with in seeking to accelerate these processes of development. What are we trying to transmit and what do we surmise that the ultimate effect of this transmission will be on the lives of the people who receive technical assistance? In short, I want to ask the question: *Development: For What?* For in all of the swiftly growing literature on the subject of assistance to the developing countries, there is rarely to be found any more than an oblique reference to this most important question.

Alexander Leighton is feeling after this question when, in the introduction to E. H. Spicer's pioneering case book on *Human Factors in Technological Change,* Leighton has a moment of philosophical reflection where he queries the morality of one country's emissaries attempting to manipulate the human beings of another country and culture. E. H. Spicer himself, although he quite readily shoulders the responsibility involved in such manipulation, nevertheless also feels constrained to supply an analogy that might give any sensitive "developer" some long second thoughts,

Changing people's customs is an even more delicate responsibility than surgery. When a surgeon takes up his instruments, he assumes the responsibility for a human life. On his skill and judgment during each moment of an operation depends the future of one individual. If the surgeon is not aware of the possibilities for good and for harm that lie in the manipulation of his scalpel, he may work irreparable damage.[1]

And Spicer is aware that in the case of the "developer," the harm or good is not, as with the surgeon, to a single individual but to the well-being and happiness of whole generations of men and women.

I have often wondered if one of the principal reasons why the study of these human objectives of development is so neglected by the writers in the more developed countries is perhaps the fact that to carry it out with any thoroughness would inevitably involve us in an agonizing reappraisal of our own human goals, of our own value systems, and of our

1. E. H. Spicer, ed., *Human Problems in Technological Change* (New York, 1953), p. 13.

own state of inward development or the lack of it. All of this can be so comfortably avoided if we can simply assume that our Western pattern of the widespread affluent life is what the developing countries are yearning for and that the technological apparatus will assure them of this if we put it into their hands.

It may seem enough to let the recipients of the development aid worry about these questions and to let these recipients reject or condition aid in terms of how they think it would affect them. But the giver of aid cannot so readily evade facing the issue of the real human objective of the development program. For at least until now, the giving countries are not giving in costly enough measure to even begin to take on the proportions adequate to the task, even if it were proved to be worth doing; nor are they really deeply involved in the issue of a major mobilization of their resources for this task.[2] And it is doubtful that we can ever become genuinely engaged and committed until we are profoundly convinced that what is being undertaken can be justified in terms of an achievable human goal that we inwardly approve of, and that it is a human goal which the recipients of this development program also accept. Only then will there be a source of motivation on which to draw to make these programs assume a central place in the nation's effort.

What then are we about in these development programs? What do we seek at bottom to bring about in the human equation of the people who make up the countries to which we go? What will be the norm by which we will judge whether or not the work has succeeded? What are we aiming to do?

I have an elder daughter who has long had a habit of demanding that her father state his presuppositions or assump-

2. Paul Hoffman of the United Nations Development Fund insists that two billion dollars a year for the next decade is necessary to help the developing countries increase their production by 25 per cent.

tions before he proceeds with any case, and I will try first of all to set down at least a few of the presuppositions which I find underlying a discussion of the objectives of development.

I. *We Are Already Involved with Each Other*

In the first place it is important to note that there is a vast and intricate process of cultural and economic interpenetration already at work that we cannot reverse. The means of communication that facilitate the exchange of news, of travelers, of one another's products is so advanced that we have to take this as given in the situation. As far back as ten years ago, I traveled on a DC-3 of Air France into a remote section of what was then French Equatorial Africa where no roads existed, and at the first air strip I was joined in my double seat by a barefooted African woman with a load that she carried on her head up to the airplane door. As I helped her latch her seat belt, in reply to my question in French as to whether this was her first trip on such a plane, she replied quietly that it was not the "premier fois" but the "deuxieme." Even if we should want to start the development process at a different point from the existing one, and to join with the Vermont farmer who declared that if "I wanted to go to Montpelier, I wouldn't start from here," we could not do it. For we do not have the choice of where we start from. We are already in this condition of interpenetration and we *must* start from here.

II. *Able But Unwilling?*

The second presupposition that I make is that for the first time in world history, the technological tools are at hand to make actually possible the placing of a minimum floor under the elemental human requirements of food, shelter, medical care, and education if these technological tools are adequately used. This does not mean that we are even remotely approaching such a condition, for over 80 per cent of the world's population receives less than $500 per person a year, and in China and India with a combined population of well over a billion, the per capita level is nearer to $60 a year. This "blanket of poverty," this "hunger curtain," is still over most of mankind. But a further factor has emerged. The mass of mankind knows that its poverty is no longer necessary. Through direct contact and through all kinds of media of communication, they have become aware of the living standards of the favored countries of the world (Russia and Czechoslovakia are now on the $500 per capita line), and they demand that they move out of their misery and want and that this happen in a forseeable time. This second fact has made the affluent countries realize that they can no longer conceal their favored home status but that a widespread awareness of their plenty is now open to all.

There is a story in Olive Schreiner's *Dreams* of a beautiful banquet table decked with the finest of linen, silver, and flowers and loaded down with every choice delicacy of food. The table was placed in a canvas enclosure and a mass of starving people had gathered around it and were pushing their hands under the canvas and begging for food. In order to protect the guests from this intrusion, guards on the inside, equipped with oaken staves, brought these down sharply on the begging hands and compelled them to withdraw. But in the present situation, there is no longer any concealment. The canvas drops are rolled up and all in the world can see precisely what the other uses for his enjoyment and well-being. This has had a dual effect: It has caused those who are in want to demand that their needs be met and met now, and it has given a bad conscience to those who are affluent; it has made them uneasy that their conspicuous consumption will ultimately carry with it a terrible judgmental toll of hate unless they respond to the world's need with an effort beyond anything that has yet appeared.

Nicolai Berdyaev has a word that might well become a proverb for our time: "Bread for myself is an economic problem. Bread for my brother is a spiritual problem." In the present situation, it is the spiritual problem of willingness, not the economic problem of ability, to help the developing nations which is the real issue.

There is always present in such situations, where peoples are able but unwilling to help to balance the budget, a kind of inwardly shriveling fourth-dimensional penalty which one of the Psalms expresses better than any word I know: "He gave them their heart's desire, but he sent withall a leanness into their soul."[3] When the situation and scope of the "Lend-Lease" mobilization of resources to Britain and Russia in World War II is thought of and the degree of our present concern and commitment for development is compared to this, the incredible modesty of our present caring is disclosed in a way that may well compel us to turn our heads away. *Able* but still largely *unwilling* is the only honest verdict that could be rendered in regard to our present token contributions of either men and women or material to this cause of assisting a massive break-through on the part of the developing nations.

III. *Communism As An Alternative Sponsor Of Development*

The third presupposition which has been hidden from many Americans and that needs to be faced with great frankness is that, whether we like it or not, there is an *ethos* in communism. Fiercely secular though it may be, this ethos in communism has the will to pass on the technological capacity to meet the basic economic needs of men to the develop-

3. Psalms 106:15.

ing countries. In its burning urgency, it is bent on sparing nothing to get this done in record time.

The food shortages that Communist China is experiencing have not come primarily from crop failures. They are the result of the total mobilization of the agricultural population of China to provide a capital structure for heavy industry, as well as to build vast dams that will not only provide power for heavy industry but water for irrigation systems and barriers for water control. Instead of too little and too late, this fierce, humanly ruthless, forced-draft system intrudes an attempt at too much and too soon. The horrible 1933 toll of starvation that took millions of lives in Russia, the overpressing of the rural population in Poland that led to the revolts in 1956, all make 1960-62 China a rerun of an old pattern. Yet none of this should blind us to the presence of an ethos to create a great industrial apparatus, to modernize a people overnight, and to create capital for a poor people by the forced-saving of rationed food, low wages, and pouring 25-30 per cent of the annual national income into investment in these technological facilities. It is only the naïve who are assured that this system will in the end break down. If you are willing to pay the terrible human price of generations of such a ruthless involuntary mobilization and of the commandeering of every human resource and to accept totalitarian patterns which direct this program, the Communist method presents a real crash program that can change the face of a poor country. It can create a substructure of the kind that can meet the basic economic needs of these people. Barbara Ward sums it up in saying that "Communism is a sort of a resumé of the revolutions that make up modernization and it offers a method of applying them speedily to societies caught fast in the dilemmas of transition."[4]

There is, then, a rival method for bringing about the

4. Barbara Ward, *The Rich Nations and the Poor Nations* (New York, 1962), p. 61.

transmission of technical development and one that has a certain ethos in it which we are compelled to acknowledge. To harassed leaders of developing countries who have gone through the glamorous and uniting period of throwing off the colonial power and of achieving political independence, but who then face the grim realities of rebuilding the economic life of their country with a minimum of outside financial assistance, there will be no small attraction to this rival method with its self-assured tough answers to all questions and its authoritarian encouragement to put down all troublesome opposition. Nicolai Berdyaev has an apt word in his book *Slavery and Freedom* which either colonial officials or the new company of anticolonial national leaders might well ponder. "It is easy for a slave to become a master; it is easy for a master to become a slave; it is almost impossible for either to become a free man."

IV. *The Development Process and Human Dignity*

Now the fourth presupposition is one that I can best introduce by quoting something which Vinoba Bhave is reported to have said to a group of Indian Communists in his audience in a village in the Indian state of Hyderabad in the course of his first proposal of the land-gift program.

You communists who have been liquidating land owners and distributing their land to the poor. . . . you are, I frankly acknowledge it, 'Mothers of the poor'. But you are bad Mothers. For in meeting the needs of the poor, you are unleashing a reign of violence in this country which will destroy the souls of the people and will lead eventually to an irresponsible tyranny. There must be another way.

And with this he proposed his symbolic land-begging from landlords, appealing to them to return a part of their land to the poor.

Now this symbolic land-gift program, although it collected

some five million acres, had grave limitations from the very outset, but it got at the real problem in a way that I am convinced we, too, must approach it. It acknowledged frankly that there is an ethos in communism, in this instance a passion to get something done about the present inequity in land ownership. But in rejecting that way, Bhave does not stop. He goes on experimentally to propose another way, and is willing to give a piece of his life to carry out the other way. At this point my fourth assumption comes into focus. Not only is there one other way than the communist way, but there are in fact many other ways of meeting these basic needs. This plurality of ways of approach can take account of the cultural and human resources of the country facing the change and can be gauged to meet its individual needs in creative directions which the Communist forced-draft system refuses even to consider.

But my fourth assumption does not end in a plea for the acknowledgment of a pluralistic or pragmatic approach to the passing on of the technical tools of development. Even more essential is the focus upon the method of introducing these technical changes. When an agricultural development officer encourages research in the form of a thousand plots on Indian farms where the farmer and his neighbors are involved, the research process has itself become a tool of education and the farmers emerge with a new confidence in their worth and in their vocation. Now it is a case of "Find out what they are doing and help them to do it better. Study their needs and help them to help themselves." It is an attempt to help them become convinced that it is possible by self-help to reach another level of productivity.

My fourth assumption presupposes that this method of introducing technical changes must *itself* do much to enhance the dignity of those who take it on; that this method itself must be an educational process that will leave the people not only with the technical tools but with a greater sense of their own dignity and confidence and trust in each other and with a sense of their responsibility for those in their country or region who are in a worse condition than their own.

In some ways this fourth presupposition is aimed at the very bull's-eye of our question—*Development: For What?* For it insists that in the course of helping these people take over the technological apparatus which can enable them to meet their minimal economic needs, the very process of this take-over shall deepen their sense of their own worth and of their responsibility in turn to work for those of their own people who are in even greater need than they are themselves. Among all of the features that may be distinctive in the open society's sponsorship of technical assistance, none stands out more prominently than this use of the very process of development to deepen the sense of dignity and independence and responsibility among the peoples of the developing countries.

Barbara Ward adds an important proviso to the accent of this fourth presupposition: an insistence that it cannot be used to cover up a halfhearted indifference to the resolution of the problems of the developing countries.

Our societies are plural in thought, plural in their ideals, plural in their ways of approaching reality. . . . We cannot therefore emulate the communist who comes and says 'Listen to me and I can tell you what to do.' Now insofar as this hesitation springs from genuine uncertainty about methods, it is honest and can be met by greater effort to discover what the answers are. But if it simply reflects the fact that we have little sense of urgency about the developing areas and have not given them the hard thought they deserve, then we can take no credit for our 'pragmatisms.' It is simply another name for indifference.[5]

V. *Development and Vital Interaction*

My fifth and final presupposition is that if our emissaries can carry through this process of sharing the technological apparatus in the context of an educational experience, they

5. *Ibid.*, pp. 65, 84.

will themselves be changed in the process and they will help create a climate in which the countries initiating the aid may be themselves immeasurably enriched by absorbing the gifts of the developing countries that have been assisted. I am not thinking alone of Christian Herter's proposal[6] for a Point V program of "what can we learn from you?" which would invite the aided countries to assist us with their discoveries and their experts as he points out they have already done in fascinating and little-acknowledged gifts of drug sources, meat tenderizers, important new tree species that may revolutionize any timber industry and the rest, or by the loan of their entomologists and medical research specialists to help us get atop of some of our most critical problems. I am thinking as well of the creation of the kind of climate that can make for that kind of exchange in which we may be profoundly enriched by the inward secrets of the people we have been closely associated with in these aid programs. Laurens Van der Post has been prominently associated with trying to open the mind and the heart of the West to such inward treasures in the African culture and temperament.

If this kind of mutual irradiation by each others' values and discoveries in a profoundly mutual educational venture were the context in which the passing over of this technological apparatus could be carried out, then we should be poised on the brink of one of the most exciting periods of all history. We might be open, perhaps for the first time, genuinely to communicate with each other. For until now such communication was rendered almost impossible so long as the complacent "colonial" mentality of cultural superiority persisted or so long as the basic needs of one of the parties were so far from being met. It is not true that you can really communicate only when you have come into a condition where you have met that need sufficiently so that you may really speak to each other and ask the life-altering questions

6. *This Week*, July 15, 1962, pp. 4-5, 14-15.

of each other—exchange pictorial art, exchange science, exchange religion, exchange music, crafts, students, builders—in short, create the climate of true peace? For true peace is not only the absence of war. True peace is vital interaction. And it is the possibility, in the course of this transmission of the technological tools, of experiencing this mutual irradiation at every level which makes this process and this epoch in history almost without parallel.

My own suspicion is that our time will either learn how to do this or we shall perish locked in a world embrace of extermination; we shall either usher in a period of mutual enrichment and stimulation that surpasses anything we have ever known, or we shall wantonly bring down the curtain both on ourselves and on the vast populations of the world whose eyes have just caught the first glint of new dawn for themselves.

VI. *Some Side-Effects of Western Industrial Society*

Now on the basis of these five assumptions I should like to raise a few of the unpleasant questions that come to development program planners and workers in their midnight hours when the public relations department is off duty, when the defenses are down and the masks are off. I want to raise a few of these devastating questions even if they seem to query or to undermine some of the very assumptions which I have just set down. In my own ignorance, I do not have the answers to most of these questions, but even to formulate a few of them may be no small service to the cause of programs of development.

One of the first and most persistent of these questions and doubts that haunt an honest development worker is that at bottom we just do not know how the blood transfusion from one society to another is creatively to be carried out. In development projects, we have not even begun to solve the blood-type business as we have been compelled to learn it in medicine after some highly tragic experiences. And in our abysmal ignorance of the effects upon the culture of one people of pouring in the technological achievements of another culture and of seeking to manipulate the receiving culture so that the transfusion will not be rejected, we often shudder at the possible ultimate results. We can also be quite certain that these midnight thoughts are not absent from the minds of sensitive spirits in the receiving countries as well, and that it is not just "Communists" who raise them.

If the blood transfusion figure is changed to that of the miracle drugs that have been appearing on the scene in such numbers of late, the business of the side-effects of the drug is only now rising up to smite us. A woman student of mine who had spent a summer and autumn in a road building work-camp in Algeria before the war began, wrote me from there that she had just had an offer of a 20 acre farm with a dozen cows, twenty sheep, and a hundred chickens. But she went on to add that there was only one difficulty with the offer—a man went with it! It is the "what goes with it," the side-effects that often give the patient as well as the physician long thoughts about the worth of the medicine, for the old adage of the disease's being completely cured by the medicine but the patient's incidentally expiring in the process is not one with which developing countries are unfamiliar.

Growing out of this question is an intensely practical one to those who would inquire about *Development: For What?* Granted that there are violently dangerous side-effects to Western technological society, is it possible to isolate them, to minimize them, or to eliminate them entirely so that the creative aspect of technology could be transmitted without these perilous side-effects?

VII. *The Side-Effects of Greed and War*

What, then, are several typical side-effects of Western technological society that might focus this issue? One of them might be the necessity for the cultivation of the bottomless greed that has been the twin of our industrial society and that would seem to have to be forever fanned in order to make our type of society run. Elspeth Huxley, the Kenyan anthropologist and novelist, suggests that the thing about the simple spear-carrying cattle-herding Masai that makes them baffle the European people who come in touch with them is that they simply do not want anything that we have! She suggests that until you can hook these people up with the fuel pump of greed, they cannot be even remotely interested in the type of modernization which our society offers.

I was once at Kingwilliamstown in South Africa where the South African Development Board has set up a huge textile mill in order to provide employment for Africans and to train them for the textile mill work. In a talk with the British manager of the mill, he told me of his desperation in trying to run the mill with an annual labor turnover of well over 100 per cent. "I have run textile mills in China, in Japan, in India, in Egypt, but I have never had anything like this. It takes me seven or eight months to train these people and just when I get them trained and they can get on with the job, they have already earned enough money for their target, and then they quit, go home, and enjoy it for six months. When they come back, if they do, they have forgotten most of what they have learned."

This textile mill operator was expressing his bitterness at the way certain African values interfered with the production of a really committed labor force and with the smooth operation of the mill. For the African has a very great sense of the value of leisure. An American college teacher was once asked why he had chosen that profession. He said that there were three basic reasons: "June, July, and August," and the African would understand. He is used to working very hard for ten days or a fortnight during the planting season, or of enduring the most strenuous hardship on a long elephant hunt. But when this period of strain is over, he expects to rest for some weeks. The African textile worker who had earned enough for a bicycle or a set of blankets, or a bride-price, or to live in his very simple fashion for several months, felt completely justified in leaving the grim, whistle-controlled, interminable routine of the mill to go home. I asked an American industrialist what he would propose to do in a situation of that kind. He was quick to reply, "Oh, that is not any real problem. We will just put a Sears Roebuck catalogue in the hands of every African woman and the man will be persuaded to stay at work."

To make our system run, you have to arouse an almost bottomless sense of need in people. Socrates is reported to have remarked on how pleasant it was to walk through the marketplace and to see there so much that he did not want. In many of the societies into which development programs come, one of their greatest gifts is to live with little and make much of it. They need more than they have, and this must not be concealed for a moment, but are we to rob them of a life where little means much? In short, can we pass on our Western technological apparatus in such a way as to meet the minimal needs of men and women without passing on the side-effect of this accentuation of greed and of perpetual discontent?

A second side-effect of our system is the matter of WAR spelled out with capital letters. For the issue is not the small scale wars or the tribal forays that have happened periodically in history but that involved only a relatively small part of the society and did not greatly affect its larger life. It is war on a cosmic scale where all are the involuntary participants, and where world destruction is no longer a mere forensic threat. In India as in Africa, a major question either spoken or suppressed but nevertheless present in the minds of sensitive spirits is the issue "Can we have the benefit of this technological civilization of yours without your involving us in these vast wars that you are already planning?" L. S. Senghor asks whether just at the point when Africa in the postcolonial period is reaching out in faith to the West, it is to find her preparing to commit suicide.

VIII. *Can the* Vermassung *of Vast Urbanization Be Skipped?*

A third side-effect of the technological modernization which has come relentlessly in the developing countries is the centripetal pull of the people into vast cities—the swift urbanization with all of its agonies which seem to come with the introduction of modern industry. The query of many a leader in a developing country is, "Can you transmit to us the technical gifts without drawing our people so rapidly into these great mass centers and subjecting them to the process of what the Germans aptly call *Vermassung?*" Industry seems to prefer this concentration. It finds that publicly provided facilities remove the burden of furnishing these at its own expense: access to electrical power, to roads, to shipping, to water, to sewage, to a ready pool of labor, to housing, to recreational facilities, to supporting auxiliary industries, and often to markets.

One of the most dismal sights in a continent like Africa today is to witness the way in which the Africans have flocked into great cities which were hopelessly unprepared for any such inundation, and the fashion in which the lives of so many who have been herded together in the segregated African slums of the cities have been rotted out by this grim transition.

The pattern in Africa is usually one of progressive waves of influx. First the men come and come alone, leaving their families behind to give them an island of security in the communal property to which they have a claim. Living alone in these cities, the men contract other liasons. At Port Elizabeth in South Africa, a decade ago, 85 per cent of the children born in the African quarter were said to be illegitimate. When the rural wives and children do come from the bush to join their husbands, the housing is usually highly inadequate. The wife has no garden from which to feed the family, no status, and she is soon driven to seek work, and delinquency thrives among her unattended children. Prisons have to be enlarged, police systems expanded, and every type of urban crime which Western society is so familiar with simply burgeons under these circumstances.

The health toll of these swift transitions is recorded in the almost incredible statistics of hypertension, heart attacks, and ulcerated stomach conditions among urban Africans.

Is there another way of sharing the technological modernization by which this stage can be skipped? Can this be done by decentralization and the use of the cheap electrical power which the new water-powered dams of Africa and India are beginning to provide? Can it be done as E. F. Schumacher, an economist of the British Coal Board, suggests, with an eye to India, by rigging the domestic economy so that the rising Western sector does not produce "an unconquerable apathy, an atmosphere of hopeless resignation" and by demoralizing and destroying the much larger traditional domestic sector of the economy which is also being energetically improved, leave the rural masses with no alternative but to swell the invasion of the cities? "I suggest that this co-existence of the two economies (the ox-cart side by side with the jet engine) is a unique problem without parallels."[7] If there is a way to skip this Western "dehumanizing deformity" of intense urbanization, there is as yet little evidence of its practice in the developing countries of our decade.

IX. *Can the Erosion of Wider Family Ties and the Spread of Secularization Be Stemmed?*

There is a fourth side-effect which seems inseparably attached to the industrial modernization and that is the forcible

7. E. F. Schumacher, *Roots of Economic Growth* (Varanasi, India: Gandhian Institute of Studies, 1961), p. 20.

detaching of those who work in it from their sense of respon-sibility for their wider family. Until the worker becomes a self-centered individualist and drops his obligations to his wider range of relations, modern industry finds that he has no proper incentive by which he can be manipulated into becoming a maximal performer in his work. For if he is paid more, it is the rule of a collective type of society that all that he and his wife and children do not urgently require for themselves is expected to go to assist nieces and nephews and cousins to a considerable range of remoteness as far as the blood or marriage tie is concerned.

In Northern Rhodesia, mining companies complain bit-terly that their mine workers' housing accomodations and the schools which they have subsidized heavily in order to house and train the miners' own children well are hopelessly overcrowded by the vast ring of relatives who turn over their children to live with and be fed by their mining relations who are earning wages. The unending hospitality which any Afri-can who earns a wage may expect to offer to his kinsmen is another tree marked for cutting by the individualism which the industrial system seems to require.

When this self-centered or immediate-family-centered men-tality is built up in modernized employment, there comes with it almost inevitably a waning of responsibility for the aging parents. Arabs in particular feel deeply shocked at the loveless way in which Western families treat their older parents, even when public subsidization of the aged takes away most material anxiety. Peoples of the developing socie-ties ask themselves if, in order to make the new system work, there has to be such a toll taken in intimate personal rela-tions. Is the result worth the price?

A fourth example of the feared side-effects of this rapid modernization process of most development programs is the secularization that threatens to eat away religious values, im-merse people in material comforts, commit them to the "heresy of numbers," and relegate religion to a thin gloss or veneer that is only used to trim the external surface of life. An observer of African peoples notes that if a primitive man lost his soul, he died, but that in the West, we have learned how to go on living in a desouled state and to regard it as the human condition.

In talking with Islamic leaders in Egypt, this drastic secularization was one of the features of Western society which was most shattering to them. It was to have lost the capacity for spiritual expectation for anything beyond the dimension of this-world control which made them fear most the technological revolution. Neville Shute, the British novelist, in his *Round the Bend* gives a striking picture of the contrast between the tough Western adequate-for-anything aviation technician and the sensitive, perceptive, inwardly agile, God-conscious Muslim with whom he is intimately associated. These Muslim leaders, knowing how much their people need material improvement and anxious for them to get it, keep wondering if in the process they must sell their birthright for it. Can you have the advantages without the withering side-effect of secularization?

The underlying question of *Development: For What?* asks whether you can stitch a gland of a technological society (that would bring so many desperately needed benefits) into the body of another culture without producing an effect of bewildering confusion? Is there not in the end the possibility of finding that the people are left with no moving image of their own? The Japanese people for all their present prosperity are struggling desperately with this very problem today.

E. F. Schumacher, to whom I previously referred, asks the telling question,

How can the impact of the West be canalized in such a way that it does not continue to throw the (mass of the) people into apathy and paralysis? . . . It was not the power of the Spaniards that destroyed the Aztec empire but the disbelief of the Aztecs in themselves. . . . It [technical assistance] demands a deep respect for the indigenous culture of those that are to be helped—maybe even a deeper respect than is possessed by many of them themselves.[8]

He is even prepared to go so far as to say to the Buddhist spiritual leaders of Burma, "We can distinguish three economic conditions: misery, sufficiency, and surfeit. Of these, two are bad for a person, a family, or a nation—and only one, sufficiency is good. . . . If you want to become materialists follow the (surfeit) way shown by Western Economics; if you want to remain Buddhists, find your own 'Middle Way.' "[9]

George Kennan, whom most developers regard as a hopeless American conservative, has gone so far as to declare, "It is my own belief that if you change the lives of people so rapidly that the experience of the father, the wisdom of the father, becomes irrelevant to the needs of the son, you have done something dangerous—you have broken the organic bond of the family and you have created an emotional trauma in the minds of the young people."[10]

X. *On Meeting "The Revolution of Rising Expectations"*

The questions that have been raised here about what we are trying to do in development projects, about *Development: For What?* are not for the purpose of encouraging the abandonment of the effort. It would be hard to estimate what the presence of the symbol of an America with its open door to immigrants and its open opportunities for a fresh start meant to untold millions of hard-pressed people in other parts of the world during the nineteenth century. In this second half of the twentieth century with what Adlai Steven-

8. *Ibid.,* pp. 13, 38, 42.
9. *Ibid.,* p. 6.
10. "A Conversation with Kennan," *Encounter* (London), No. 78 (March, 1960).

son has called "the revolution of rising expectations" all ablaze in the world, not only America but the whole cluster of open-society countries must decide whether they are ready for the costly steps that will be necessary if they are to become a symbol of a comparable wave of hope in the world. But any serious weighing of the queries that I have raised here may profoundly alter the methods of approach, the rate of change, the type of personnel who can communicate the kind of vital interaction which is required, and the way to learn from the failures of the past.

One of America's wisest agricultural statesman, Carl C. Taylor, draws attention to the personnel side and to a largely neglected factor in the programs of development. He writes, "Is it not time that the United States really studied the extent to which the non-economic aspects of its own culture have affected its own development?" And he makes the startling suggestion about the really transforming features that an agricultural development representative may be communicating as he works in another culture.

What is it that they have to contribute that is of the greatest value? Is it their tractors, their centrifuges, their scientific concepts, the dollars in their jackets, or is it their attitude toward nature? Their willingness to risk ridicule to try a new method? Their ways of dealing with their peers, 'superiors,' and 'subordinates' within an organization? Their sense of time as a valuable asset? Their propensity to want to measure with precision? . . . Their preference for local over national government? . . . Their willingness to delegate responsibility coupled with distrust of combinations of power? Their preference of projects instead of dogma? Their acceptance of some right of equal consideration for all persons? Their concern for the under-dog? Their preference of the new to the old?[11]

Here he is exposing to view the real engagement, the vital interaction, of the value systems of two cultures which makes it highly important that the emissaries of this development

11. *Development of the Emerging Countries* (Washington, D.C.: The Brookings Institution, 1962), pp. 101, 102.

work be not only technically competent but humanly alive. For if the development is only to hand over the technological apparatus, this can also be done by a totalitarian hand. But if, in the process of handing it over, the goal is to deepen the sense of dignity and human worth and responsibility and to achieve genuine mutual stimulation, then the transmitters themselves are of peculiarly vital importance.

The worth of programs like the Peace Corps and of voluntary agencies supporting young people in small development programs is not to be tallied alone in what they may accomplish in the field during their initial residence, though this contribution is not small. Of equal weight is the fact that from the returning veterans of these groups, flexible, concerned candidates for international civil service careers and development programs can be recruited and trained. Instead of having to rely in the future for technical development personnel on the 40 to 65 year old group of domestically-rooted and often culturally-sclerotic veterans who must be bribed by premium salaries and who often leave their home countries with the greatest reluctance, a whole new increment of younger, more open, and more imaginative personnel is now in prospect. After an experience with these developing countries at first hand, their eyes may not be closed to tackling the tough enigmas which our queries about *Development: For What?* have raised, and their experimentally-minded ventures may help to answer some of the questions which in our present ignorance we can only gropingly seek to formulate.

Index